# BDSM MASTERY

*The Complete Guide for Dominants and Submissive. Earn Respect From Your Sub Has a Dom, Discover Ways to Explore Your Sexual Fantasies and Sexual Role Play Examples.*

By

**CHERRY WILSON**

Particular creators claim all copyrights not held by the distributor.

The data in this is offered for educational purposes exclusively and is all-inclusive as so. The introduction of the data is without a contract or any assurance confirmation.

The marks used shall be without consent, and the distribution of the mark shall be without the consent or support of the proprietor of the mark. All trademarks and trademarks within this book are just for explanation and Are held clearly by the owners, who are not associated with this record.

# TABLE OF CONTENTS

# INTRODUCTION

When many of us listen to the letters "BDSM," we assume of Rihanna vocal singing regarding whips and also chains or Fifty Shades' Christian Grey stating "Laters, infant,"? As well as while it's no key that the BDSM area is, emergency room, not all that warm of the Fifty Shades franchise business, there's no rejecting that the collection has actually placed the twist in the limelight.

Depending on what type of kinky individuals you talk to, this kind of horrendous dream might be appropriate on the cash, or so much from the reality that your kink-friendly discussion companion ruptureds right into giggling.

## WHAT IS BDSM, TRULY?

BDSM, which represents Bondage, Domination/Submission, Sadism, as well as Masochism, is a broad-reaching classification of bed room play that can vary from the light to wild, all depending upon what each pair locates an attractive, warm turn-on.

Individuals that frequently exercise BDSM in any type of kind (or numerous kinds!) are referred to as "lifestylers", particularly when they greatly mingle and also connect with various other BDSM enthusiasts, fre□uently developing a neighborhood of similar people that review kinky play as well as in some cases come down with various other companions or pairs.

Chains & Discipline/ Domination & entry/ Sadism & Masochism (BDSM) is a wide classification of bed room play. It can be soft or harsh depending upon what your companion takes into consideration attractive as well as a turn-on. Everybody is various and also for this really factor, it's extremely essential that you have a significant discussion and also established some limits prior to participating in any kind of act.


Individuals that exercise BDSM often in any type of types are referred to as "lifestylers", particularly if they interact socially and also communicate with various other BDSM fans. They typically create a neighborhood of similar individuals that go over subjects pertaining to BDSM and also in some cases come down with various other pairs or companions.


The BDSM tag can put on several sorts of sex-related play that drop beyond the vanilla style. Vanilla usually describes intercourse in one of the most simple way-- sans also one of the most novices' kind of twist playthings, like fuzzy manacles or a smooth blindfold. Yes, this implies that if you've ever before blindfolded your companion with a soft connection or utilized your lacy underwears to bind their hands over their head, you've participated in a light variation of BDSM.

The BDSM tag puts on several sorts of sex-related play that do not drop inside the vanilla style. Vanilla describes sexual relations in the easiest way. That being stated, any kind of type of twist playthings (also a smooth blindfold or hairy manacles) drops in the BDSM group; this indicates if you've ever before been blindfolded or utilized a soft connection to bind your companions' hands over their head, you've participated in a light variation of BDSM.

Some pairs really take pleasure in the complete Hollywood-style dungeon, total with a wood St. Andrew's Cross to bind their companion spread-eagle while they excitedly wait for an endorphin-releasing whipping. That's since BDSM rests on settlement and also authorization, as well as the sex-related variants can differ extremely from pair to pair.

In The New Topping Book, co-author Janet W. Hardy explains BDSM as "a task in which the individuals eroticize experiences or feelings that would certainly be undesirable in a non-erotic context."

Durable anxieties that BDSM is both consensual and also sensual: Pain comes to be enjoyment throughout BDSM. What's taking place might appear non-consensual without context, yet both companions are taking part in play that they're taking pleasure in-- regardless of just how embarrassing it might appear from the exterior.

"Many individuals take into consideration BDSM perverted, dehumanizing, or even worse. "In BDSM, the gamers constantly organize points in advancement with clear, intimate interaction, which develops an uni□ue sexual bond."

BDSM is eventually regarding 2 or even more individuals caring and also relying on for each other by means of sexual power plays. That's why BDSM is so appealing: All the discomfort, destruction, as well as embarrassment in BDSM is carried out in a manner in which types affection in between gamers.

Normally talking, many kinds of BDSM have 2 duties: a leading (or dom) as well as a passive (or sub). The below obtains the dom's discomfort as well as enjoyment. They're the ones obtaining whipped, defeated, as well as compelled right into those foot massage therapies.

Queer twist neighborhoods make use of "leading" as well as "lower" in referral to the dom as well as below, sticking to olden duties from the gay, lesbian, and also transgender areas. In age play, the leading is usually referred to as a "daddy dom" or "mommy domme," and also the passive is called the "little.".

There's likewise a vast range of twists as well as strategies that drop right into chains as well as self-control play, as well as they can fre uently be discovered throughout dom as well as below connections. There's rope play, which entails a dom limiting a below with rope.

Any type and all of these kinds of play are thought about BDSM. Not every BDSM professional will certainly experiment with them, naturally. They're crucial components of the BDSM umbrella, which goes to reveal simply exactly how varied play can be.

# BDSM AND CONSENT

BDSM is constantly consensual

When pairs' method energetic authorization, it implies they never ever try a sex-related act without asking initially, as well as they pay attention carefully to their companion throughout sex simply in case something that generally really feels excellent takes place to really feel negative.

There's one core truth to keep in mind concerning BDSM: It's all consensual.

Submissive as well as leading partnerships occur inside something called a play scene or play room, where 2 or even more play companions get together to pass scenes. Like function play, gamers go over the scene in advance as well as experience alternatives that a leading can participate in along with ones they wish to stay clear of.

If a dom does not desire to have any type of kind of genital call throughout play, after that it's the below's task to recognize that border. A below that desires to be spanked and also searched in a scene is involving in consensual BDSM play. A below that does not desire to be spanked must not be spanked since that's a fierce criminal activity.

BDSM's enjoyable originates from the reality that there are borders. At any moment, a play companion can □uit as well as state a risk-free word play, repair an issue, or speak about why a circumstance breached their approval. There's absolutely nothing hotter than obtaining whipped, spanked, as well as weakened by your enthusiast when you desire it greater than anything worldwide.

In BDSM, part of exercising authorization entails discussing the regards to the sex-related experience prior to any kind of clothing come off as well as candle lights are lit.

These discussed policies can be as company as, "I do not such as being spanked, so please do not ever before spank me on any kind of part of my body," or a person can determine to provide specific tasks a shot with the choice to quit the scene if they end up being uneasy, either literally or psychologically, like "Sometimes I such as being passed through with huge sex playthings, yet I've never ever attempted genital fisting prior to. Please go slow-moving, make use of great deals of lube, as well as I'll inform you to quit if I do not like it."

Due to the fact that electrifying, consensual BDSM can take lots of types, allow's consider some usual facets of this typically misconstrued sex-related specific niche that unmasks all those false and also frightening tales you've possibly listened to throughout the years. You open up your collaboration to an entire great deal of kinky enjoyable when you obtain past the reports!

## BDSM PLAY TAKES ABILITY

Like a lot of points sex-related, it takes some time as well as method to discover exactly how to sub or dom. Carolyn Yates mentions a variety of security pointers that doms demand to bear in mind to bind their belows. And also as it ends up, there's a great deal to understand when limiting your enthusiast.

" Keep the rope loose sufficient that you can function 2 fingers in between the rope and also your task companion's skin," Yates states. "The objective is to limit, not to remove flow. If the rope may splash (it's actually warm and also you're both sweating, for instance), leave it also looser."

That's since rope play teases with threat. For brand-new play companions that have really little experience with rope-tying, threat boosts.

Rope-tying isn't the only point that budding belows and also doms need to find out. They need to plan for emergency situations, like a below diminishing also much right into themselves to interact, or a dom sensation bewildered by a scene as well as re□uiring to □uit.

That's □uite regular if it takes even more than a couple of play sessions for points to truly click in between you and also your companion. Simply keep in mind to do your research study prior to entering, and also never ever attempt anything brand-new without examining it, exercising it, as well as producing a back-up strategy if something fails.

# BONDAGE

## WHAT IS BONDAGE?

When you assume of BDSM, a tied-up sharp is possibly what right away springs to mind. The B represents Bondage, and also it plays an undoubtedly significant function in a lot of lifestylers' playbooks.

Chains is an exceptionally preferred kind of BDSM fulfilment. I think this is since for those drawn in to BDSM satisfaction, chains binds the body while launching the mind-- a consistency hardly ever located in any other grown-up enjoyment task.

Chains cuffs are the most frequently understood of all chains sex playthings. For an outright newbie (as well as really, for all those delighting in chains enjoyments) I would certainly encourage preventing steel manacles. Chains cuffs may secure with Velcro or a clasp attachment.

Chains rope looks definitely stunning in detailed bindings like Shibari (a Japanese type of rope chains) yet these can be really hard for an outright novice to reproduce. If you seriously intend to attempt rope chains after that it's a good idea to likewise buy a manual on the topic-- and also have a set of safety and security scissors ready while you're practicing in case of emergency situations. Chains tape is fantastic for novices to BDSM-- easy to use and also sticks just to itself, not the body.

Incredibly limited or otherwise body-bending chains can trigger significant injury as well as lasting nerve damages if done inaccurately. We advise keeping away from the rougher things till you truly recognize what you're doing and also have actually been managed by a pro.

## WHY BONDAGE CAN BE SO MUCH FUN

Whether you're an individual or a lady, now you've most likely checked out - or at the very least become aware of - the "Fifty Shades of Grey" sensation. The fastest-selling trilogy of perpetuity shows the S&M partnership in between unblemished Anastasia Steele and also young organisation magnate Christian Grey.

Regardless of the frightening summaries you've listened to regarding chains in the room, a little twist can bring you and also your companion unlimited enjoyment and also delight in between the sheets.

Whether you simply desire to link each various other up, slap one an additional about, or go all out with nipple area clamps as well as rectal grains, chains can be your brand-new BFF in bed.

## WHY S&M?

Simply checking out those 2 words - sadism and also masochism- put alongside suffices to transform any person off of S&M. You're possibly creating mental images of a fat individual called The Gimp yanking on his chain as he eye-fucks Bruce Willis in "Pulp Fiction".

S&M can function for regular, ordinary individuals as well ... unless you've been living in a cage below a pawnshop. That was possibly The Gimp's issue.

S&M can draw out a lively side of you as well as your companion that you've never ever experienced. And also, S&M and also chains is founded on shared trust fund and also interaction, which can bring you and also your companion better with each other than ever.

### *Chains & S&M for Beginners - What You Need to Know*

An approximated one in 5 pairs meddles S&M as well as one in 20 participates in exceptionally severe duty play. To put it simply, chains is much more typical than you could believe. Prior to you go flexing your companion over a sofa, allow us offer you a quick Bondage overview.

The most crucial point to go over prior to you welcome S&M and also chains right into the bed room is limits. As we stated in the past, S&M is all concerning interaction. Prior to you obtain it on, rest down as well as have a significant conversation concerning what you desire to obtain out of S&M as well as just how much you both desire to go with it.

It's likewise essential to have a safety and security word in the bed room. This makes certain that if points obtain hefty and also warm for one of you to manage, you can simply state the security word and also take a rest.

### *Toys, Tips as well as Tricks*

Currently that you're all set to check out a little bit of S&M as well as chains in the bed room, you require to fill up on enjoyable as well as kinky playthings. If you're brand-new to every one of this, begin light and also avoid the face masks, bull whips and also genital rounds.

Begin with fuzzy manacles or rope, a tickler as well as a blindfold or little plant. You can normally obtain an established with every one of these consisted of. Starting with lighter, spirited playthings allows you as well as your companion to accustom yourselves to them in the bed room and afterwards go on to extra major gizmos if you so pick.

On the initial number of evenings, simply trying out linking each other up and also locating your private convenience degrees. If you like being linked up or doing the controling, pay focus to. And also make certain to interact every little thing you are believing as well as really feeling.

### *Chains Moves Not for the Faint of Heart*
The even more you and also your companion discover S&M as well as chains, the a lot more you'll agree to evaluate your borders. For those of you that intend to press the limits, there are lots of strong steps that S&M as well as chains deals.

Round tricks are an enjoyable method of maintaining your companion quiet. If you utilize one, be certain to come up with a hand motion or signal that suggests you desire out - you will not be able to utter your safeword.

Blending discomfort as well as satisfaction is absolutely sexual as well as will certainly make for a eruptive as well as extreme climax. Including a little bit of function play to the shenanigans is likewise a fantastic concept.

### Chains Bringing You Closer

Not a great deal of individuals would certainly believe that paddling as well as hog linking your husband would certainly enhance your connection, however it truly can.

Ladies particularly hesitate that permitting a companion to connect them up as well as control them in the bed room will certainly play out in the remainder of their connection, however this is not real whatsoever. S&M is purely booked for the room, as well as guys that intend to have control over their sweethearts in reality have power problems that ought to be attended to by a therapist.

S&M and also chains will certainly raise the depend on and also confidence you have in one an additional and also open doors you never ever believed existed, consisting of one to better sex-related enjoyment if done right.

Rope chains uses all the creative thinking as well as versatility a kinky mind can ever before desire, specifically when you take into consideration all the ropes offered.

While you enjoy the sensation of chains, you could be discovering that the present chains fast remedies out there aren't aiding you attain the excellent, placement that you as well as your companion had in mind. That's where rope comes in.

Rope chains is distinct in that it permits you to limit your companion in any type of method feasible. Inspect out the job of Shibari or Kinbaku rope creates to see simply exactly how versatile rope can be. Desire to obtain right into rope chains?

### Safety and security

Currently that I've obtained you all thrilled, you could be assuming regarding the rope area you've seen at the e□uipment shop. The textile isn't dealt with for human skin. A lot more usually than not, you'll finish up having to reduce the rope right into items simply to eliminate it (commonly from a very-agitated companion).

Rather, choose a rope that's especially created for human chains. Human chains rope can conveniently be discovered online or at a regional sex store. They look like scissors yet are made to securely reduce apparel or plasters (and also, in this situation, chains rope) from an individual's skin without reducing or scratching them.

When buying rope, do not fail to remember concerning discovering just how to utilize it. While there are several on the internet overviews that offer detailed guidelines to particular rope connections, you might favor to get a publication to go together with your brand-new chains acquisition.

Since you understand just how much enjoyable rope chains can be as well as several of the security points to fret about, it's time to get your very first item of rope. With every one of the choices available, however, exactly how do you understand which one to ac□uire? When you're looking for your initial item, believe regarding some of these points.


### Dimension Matters

The most vital element of any type of item of chains rope is the size of the rope. While you can constantly connect 2 items of rope with each other, it's generally much less inconvenience to have the appropriate size you re□uire in the very first area.

### Does Thickness

Along with size, density is an additional vital element of chains rope. Where a big, thick rope may be difficult to utilize on a penis, thinner ropes would certainly be uneasy for usage on the human body.

### Consider Bondage Rope Material

Along with the cleansing as well as companion factors to consider provided below, it likewise makes a distinction to the feeling of the rope. Nylon often tends to be elastic and also soft while a hemp rope might really feel scratchy as well as harsh. If you're much more right into the suggestion of a kinky, harsh rope scene, you might favor hemp or hemp.

### Know How You'll Use Your Bondage Rope

The rope that will certainly be appropriate for suspension will certainly be various than a rope that's appropriate for flooring connections. If your connections on a regular basis consist of nude chains or rope operating near physical li□uids, you may desire to pick a rope that's very easy to clean.

### *Contemplate Who You'll Use It With*

You might not re□uire to stress regarding cleansing the rope after every usage if you do not obtain it untidy if you just prepare on utilizing this rope with one individual. For short-term chains that has you binding several individuals, take into consideration obtaining a rope that's simpler to take and also clean treatment of to guarantee you're looking after your companions.

### *Think of Cleaning*

If you're one of those individuals as well, you possibly do not desire to select a hemp rope that calls for hand replacing the rope as well as cleaning's material after every laundry. Some individuals locate the rope care-taking procedure to be a type of intimate link in itself, so you'll require to identify what jobs best for you.

### *Identify Your Color*

As soon as you've figured out whatever else concerning your rope, it's time to believe concerning the rope's shade. Think about obtaining different shades in a pair various sizes to make □uite creates together with your detailed rope job. Producers have actually made rope in an entire rainbow of shades--

consisting of glow-in-the-dark alternatives as well as vivid neons.

Bear in mind, if you ever before determine to transform your passion in rope chains right into an extreme love, you'll begin to figure out what help you as you proceed your expedition. Anticipate your rope bag to constantly alter and also change as you discover your very own enjoys and also choices. The 25-foot pink nylon rope you presently have might not be the rope that you like to utilize in 5 years, yet it'll constantly have a soft spot in your heart.

What's vital is that you appreciate the trip. You can constantly get a lot more rope if it does not benefit what you wanted, yet valuing your brand-new pastime as well as your companion's participation goes a long way towards con□uering a few of those discouraging rope speed bumps. Anticipate to be purchasing even more rope once again quickly in the future, and also appreciate the trial and error that will certainly obtain you to that factor!

## THE DO'S AND DON'T OF ROPE BONDAGE

Why play with rope when there are simpler and also faster methods to bind a person? Some delight in the close to unlimited adaptability rope chains offers, considering that you can twist your companion right into simply concerning any type of setting the body will certainly enable.

Play on if you're being threat conscious as well as everybody is appreciating themselves. That's a huge if. Rope can be lots of and also stealthily straightforward individuals begin having fun with rope prior to they understand just how to do so securely.

This area will certainly provide you a short introduction of the security issues related to rope play as well as some concepts to get going. Absolutely nothing takes the area of hands-on knowing. I highly recommend you look for out rope teams in your location if you desire to end up being completed at rope chains.

### The Rules of Rope: Safety

There are a couple of fundamental points to look out for when you're playing with rope or involving in any kind of kind of chains. Maintain the canine collar regulation in mind: make certain you can glide one or 2 fingers in between the body as well as the rope component being bound, specifically when linking wrists. (If rope isn't your point, there are lots of super-safe, easy chains packages.).

This can take place in the methods you would certainly anticipate, like having limited rope around the upper body, however you additionally have to look out for positional asphyxiation. Bonus treatment requires to be taken when utilizing settings such as the hog-tie and also any type of setting that brings the upper body and also knees with each other.

When attempting anything brand-new, particularly chains, maintain open interaction with your companion. Do not have fun with tricks at the same time. Make certain you're signing in regularly, as well as validating your companion can take a breath well, which none of their arm or legs are going tingly or numb.

When you're going to make use of rope for chains, have EMT sheers within arm's reach at all times. If your companion re□uires to be cost-free of the rope right away, you require to be able to reduce it promptly.

It's finest to exercise chains on the ground or on the bed, particularly prior to you understand just how you'll respond to being in rope. Some individuals are prone to passing out as well as an autumn can create injury.

Beware of rope from the regional e□uipment shop, as much of it is also rigid or not skin pleasant. Your finest wager is rope made particularly for chains.

One of the wonderful points regarding rope chains is that the structure obstructs you find out as a newbie never ever shed their efficiency. They just come to be parts of even more challenging and also sophisticated chains. One of the standard structure blocks for nearly any kind of kind of rope chains is the solitary column connection.

Much of rope chains involves the control as well as circulation of the rope, so attempt to manage the trap a manner in which optimizes performance. A lot of designs of rope chains make use of an item of increased rope, beginning with the bight (the center of the rope.).


**Locking up Your Partner.**
Draw out regarding an arm's size of rope and also curtain it over the column to be.

Cover the running end of the rope (the one with the bight) around the arm or leg a number of times. 3 covers appears to be suitable for convenience. The broader the covers, the better the location over which stress will certainly be dispersed.

Cross the running end over the covers.

Next off, draw the running end below all the covers (in between the arm or leg as well as the rope.) Now, you just connect the running as well as standing ends with each other. There are numerous methods to do this, however the easiest method is to develop a loophole in the lengthy end of the rope (the standing end) by turning it in towards your covers.

Draw the bight with and also tighten up down. (Depending on just how unsafe your rope is, you might re□uire to include an additional fifty percent drawback or overhand knot to make.

When it's drawn on, the essential point to look out for with any kind of chains connection is that it does not tighten up down on the arm or leg. Be certain to inspect on your connections consistently if you're going to have somebody in chains for a while.

## BONDAGE IS MORE THAN JUST ROPE

Do you like to be linked up, or do you favor to be the one doing the connecting? Whether you're right into the entire BDSM scene or not, chains is an enjoyable method to obtain kinky. Chains is so a lot even more than simply rope.

Have a look at a couple of choices for chains. Mix as well as suit, attempt what interest you, and also have some kinky enjoyable in the process.

### *Having fun with Rope*

Of program, if we're going over chains, rope should have a reference. Of all, allow me state, I'm the one being linked up in my connection, not the various other method around.

With rope, you can obtain as basic or as made complex as you like: from a straightforward knot connecting your companion to the bed to the intricacies of Japanese chains. Chains fans might discuss the definitions, however Japanese chains is usually a mix of charm as well as sexiness. It needs persistence on the component of the base being bound as well as method from the leading functioning with the rope.

### *Quick and also Easy Tie Ups*

OK, so you're right into the suggestion of being or limiting limited, however all that rope job seems like ... well, job. Perhaps you like rope, however often you re⬜uire something quicker and also much easier. No concerns, you have alternatives.

I have a roll of purple chains tape resting in my plaything box right currently, pleading to be utilized. Excellent chains tape ought to hold well, come off the skin ⬜uickly, and also not harm also a lot as it comes off.

No kind of chains need to reduce off blood circulation-
- purple hands show an actual issue. Alternatives are
bondage cuffs that are made of natural leather or
various other products connected in the.


### *The Softer Side of Restraint*

In the state of mind for something softer and also
much more sensuous? Being consolidated headscarfs
as well as silk connections can make greater than
simply your mouth water. They're likewise a much less
harmful means to present chains right into your
connection since they're a great deal much less
challenging than steel, and even natural leather.

Ties and also headscarfs can play several functions in
the bed room. Possibly your hands are connected with
each other, over your head. Your companion could do
anything they desire to you, as well as you're
powerless ... Whew, is it obtaining cozy in below?

Headscarfs, connections as well as also underwears are
a sensual method to bind somebody's feet or hands.
The gentleness of the textile reduces the possibility of
injury. And also, it's a non-threatening method to limit
your companion, have your means with them
(consensually obviously), and also have fun with
chains.

## *Honor Bondage*

Honor chains does not entail playthings in any way. It's seen frequently in D/s connections or BDSM scenes, however it does not just take place there. It's a quite easy idea also.

One companion informs the various other to hold a placement-- hands behind back, stooping on the flooring, bent over, you select. The various other companion does not relocate, no issue what.

What collections recognize chains apart from various other chains play is that it needs the base or passive to proactively limit themselves. For a couple of hrs of kinky play, it's the least costly as well as, in my viewpoint, one of the most sensual kinds of chains.


## *Pervertibles*

I desired to consist of an area on pervertibles in chains due to the fact that I understand what it's like to live on a spending plan. Pervertibles are day-to-day products repurposed for kinky play.

In chains, you have a couple of choices. Rope, cables, chains as well as cable televisions can all be bought from your regional house renovation shop, occasionally for simply dimes per foot. Velcro can work as manacles as well as various other chains alternatives.

There are some benefit to purchasing for chains playthings in a trusted sex store. Due to the fact that pervertibles are created for chains, they might not be that risk-free either. Constantly have safety and security scissors convenient when you're linking somebody up, as well as never ever neglect your companion's safety and security in your thrill to obtain kinky.

Invest a great deal of time discovering just how to bind or link a person securely. Never ever fail to remember the aftercare when you're done.

## BONDAGE AND DISABILITY (WORKING AROUND ABILITIES IN PLAY)

When taking part in chains play with a person with handicaps, those specials needs can confirm to be a difficulty. That isn't to state that points will certainly go incorrect, however any kind of possible threat to a companion have to be thought about. The great information is that in numerous instances, kinky play with an impaired companion is simply like kinky play with any kind of various other individual: It calls for treatment, interaction and also permission.

### Love and also Learn

Ask your companion what you re□uire to view out for associated to the impairment. This is particularly crucial when it comes to undetectable impairments or problems. Also if your companion simply has bronchial asthma, you might still desire to discover what you can do to assist them in instance of a bronchial asthma assault throughout a play session.

### Talk It Out

Interaction goes together with education and learning. Talking of rope, you might have to change usual connections to suit your companion. Interact with your companion concerning just how they would certainly such as check-ins to happen (Speaking?

### Play Safe

Have safety and security scissors on hand to rapidly reduce totally free any type of rope and also not damage skin; have any type of clinical tools needed depending on the certain re□uirements of your companion. You might additionally desire to have a covering or preferred thing useful, not simply for very first help as well as security, yet likewise to integrate right into aftercare for the sensory convenience

These pointers all interact to guarantee your play remains attractive as well as secure for everybody. Make certain to take your companion's hand as well as go over these essential problems, able bodies or not.

## WANT TO TIE UP YOUR PARTNER? HERE'S HOW TO TELL THEM

It's a wintertime's day, I'm 23 years of ages, and also trembling.

Not from the cool, however from the ideas flying via my head, all overlooked desires; and also I'm with a woman with brilliant red hair and also the bluest eyes that I've ever before seen. Due to the fact that I desire really seriously to ask her something, however am frightened that as soon as I do, she will certainly run off as well as never ever talk to me once again. We were currently starting to bring up physical affection, yet what I desired from her ... well, it had actually been pierced right into me time and also once again that you did not bring it up.

All I desire to do is take this lady back to my area, strip off some of her garments, and also link her up. Absolutely nothing surrounding on extreme BDSM; no whips or chains, candle light wax, or also infiltration.

This was, in component, due to the fact that I feared her response, and also in component since I can listen to the voices of my family members specifically advising me that such points were revolting, as well as that I need to be embarrassed of myself.

For a great deal of individuals, bringing up the intro of chains, spirited and also light ventures with silk rope as well as lavish blindfolds, can appear an overwhelming job. Whether it's concern of denial, concern of being classified as in some way perverted, or also worry of approving and also articulating our dreamed-up situations with others, the subject of delighting proclivities can make also the finest of us flush, laugh nervously, or drink like a teen attempting to chat to their crush.

### What Talking About Bondage Really Means

When bringing up the topic of chains, you are actually asking a person to offer you their depend on, their flexibility, and also possibly their suggestion of security in exchange for sensual/sexual enjoyment, power-play, and also a feasible re-evaluation of your very own connection. By asking a person you care regarding to allow you control them, also in the most risk-free and also considerate of means, you are asking for their trust fund, as well as revealing that you feel you've gained the right to discover it.

Think of for a minute that your companion is asking you to take component in a workout where they desire to limit you. Do you desire them to be frightened, sweating, breathing heavily, or evading around the topic, or would certainly you like something simple, considerate as well as, most importantly, familiar with what they are asking? Exactly how would certainly you respond to either scenario?

To this day, it's the hardest component of locating brand-new companions or presenting the suggestion of chains to my existing companions. You can also ask my companion, Lily, since she obtained a whole lot of these tossed her method when we initially fulfilled.

### It's Just Elaborate Foreplay

We border fetish play with such an air of aura and also power that we have a tendency to neglect that it's actually simply one more component of being intimate, as well as it's one method that several possible companions are a lot more than eager to experiment with. Bring it up that method. Be open concerning what you desire to do, and also why you desire to do it.

### Begin Slow

Those ideas are constantly there in brand-new individuals, also if they urge they're great with it as well as not frightened or daunted. You require to take that initial session gradually, and also be conscious of your companion since they will most definitely allow you understand if they appreciate what's taking place ... or not.

I found out that the tough method with one of my companions. (Get even more novice pointers in Why Bondage Can Be So Much Fun.).

### Inquire What They Want.

Possibly you're gladdened that your companion concurred, or you're taking their acceptance as permit to delight your inmost needs, however take the time out to see what they understand regarding chains, as well as just how ideal to mix your wishes with their own. Possibly they would certainly never ever believed regarding it previously, or possibly they were maintaining a comparable trick from you, however you require to establish that usual ground prior to ever before acting on it.

### Anxiety Is the Mind Killer

Concern can eliminate any kind of need, damage any type of form of depend on, or change something beautiful right into something uneasy in no time level. Think me when I state that worry can trigger you to entirely tune out whatever around you, and also that fear that you're doing something incorrect can extremely □uickly lead you to doing something extremely incorrect since you're concentrated on the incorrect points.

### Be Desire-less, Be Excellent, Be Gone

When it comes to presenting something like chains right into a partnership, all you can do is ask, pay attention to your companion as well as execute together with what they desire. There's no magic bullet that can make every little thing occur the means you desire it to. All you can do is be your outright ideal, offer your companion the ideal experience you can, and also be prepared for what occurs after that.

You appreciate them sufficient to ask if they desire to be component of it. That goes a lengthy method in developing the count on essential to develop something lovely.

When I initially brought the concept of chains play up with Lily, we were resting in a resort space in Portland in between occasions at a seminar. I desired to see her kneeling, with her wrists linked behind her back. 2 years after that, we have actually created an extreme connection that is just improved by chains play.

Keep in mind, it's simply chains.

## STEPS TO CHOOSING BONDAGE RESTRAINTS

Chains permits some individuals to really feel enjoyment in means they never ever understood was feasible. It's a extremely intimate as well as brand-new experience with one more individual

Currently that you've chosen you desire to attempt chains, you might really feel a little bit shed in terms of what restrictions would certainly be excellent for you and also your companion. There are fairly a couple of options out there, yet we desire to make certain you finish up with something that makes your future and also initial experiences definitely ideal.

Simply comply with these 6 actions to selecting chains restrictions. There's no incorrect means to utilize these actions. (Not persuaded that chains is for you?

### Consider the Size of Your Cuffs

Some wrist and also chains cuffs come in different dimensions (tiny, tool, big). A collection of cuffs that fits the wrists might not fit the ankle joints, so take into consideration determining those

### Determine the Possibility of Escape

Some individuals truly enjoy the experience of "not being able to leave," however others will certainly not be able to absolutely loosen up unless they understand they can obtain out of their cuffs if re□uired. If you would certainly such as a very easy means to get away, look for cuffs with Velcro attachment. If you would certainly such as cuffs that are not so very easy to obtain out of, look for cuffs that use securing fastenings.

### Know Your Anchor Points

Just how do you prepare on utilizing your chains cuffs? A lot of individuals typically desire to utilize them for their made objective of restriction. Several restrictions include a solitary O-ring for restriction functions, yet uni□ue cuffs might come or have several o-rings outfitted with clips to connect the cuffs to each various other.

### Contemplate a Beginner's Bondage Set

If you have not made use of chains restrictions prior to after that you may take into consideration ac□uiring an established developed for novices. These collections are normally extremely cost effective and also consist of beginner-friendly chains things such as wrist restrictions, ankle joint restrictions, a blindfold, a collar, a chain, as well as some kind of effect plaything (such as a flogger or a plume).

### Enjoy a Matching Set

Some restrictions and also chains devices are made in matching color pattern with matching styles by the producer. They are normally bought individually unlike the boxed novice's collections. You may desire to maintain the shade as well as pattern in mind while buying your playthings if you're a person that favors an excellent aesthetic result.

### Think About Special Features

When you've figured out the essentials, you'll desire to assume concerning any type of uni☐ue functions you would certainly like to see in your restrictions. Some restrictions are crafted with additional cushioning and also handle-holds for suspension chains. Look at uni☐ue enhancements to make certain your chains dream comes real.

Currently that you have an excellent suggestion concerning what to look for in your restrictions, take your concepts directly to your favored plaything seller! Why not acquire a pair of your last selections as well as locate out, first-hand, specifically what issues to you?

Water chains: It's hot and also damp - what's not to enjoy? Water chains takes whatever that's enjoyable regarding chains and also includes it right into an exhilarating water setting for an added little bit of mischievous allure.

Water chains does not just consist of restrictions. You can make use of any kind of kind of water-safe chains thing such as tricks, belts, collars, and also various other chains devices. If it integrates some kind of BDSM aspect, it possibly certifies as "water chains."

If the suggestion of being soaked undersea by your companion and being held there completely under their control sounds like your hottest fantasy, then water bondage can do that for you. While many people play on the lighter side of things with water bondage, it can also include more intense types of play like being sprayed with water or dunked under water.

### *Security First ...*

Like any type of BDSM task, you ought to understand the dangers included as well as take actions to handle those threats. Water chains, greater than lots of various other tasks, calls for much more interest to prospective threat. You're mixing the pleasures of restraint with the fun of an a□uatic environment.

Before either you or your partner even thinks about getting into the water, you should both have a discussion about what fantasy you have in mind. If you are thinking of being dunked underwater and yet your partner just wants to try using bondage cuffs in the shower, neither of you will come away from the encounter feeling happy. This will limit the worry of accidental miscommunication during your water bondage scene.

The next safety issue is to ensure that everyone will have good footing and breathing ability in your water area. When using wrist bondage, it can be very hard for someone to catch themselves if they slip.

Unless you're extremely careful and are an expert with medical issues and water submersion, it's best if you avoid holding or dunking anyone underwater. Instead, stick to splashing or spraying water on your partner. If you choose to play with more intense forms of water bondage, it's very important that you both obey the safeword and understand that you created earlier.

As you can see, there are a great deal of points to think about prior to taking pleasure in water chains. Make certain you take the appropriate time to plan the security elements of your play to ensure every person strolls (or creeps, relying on exactly how extreme the climaxes are) away securely from the experience.

***Select the Right Tools***

For that factor, you'll desire chains devices that are up to the job of water play. Look for things made from neoprene.

If you wish to obtain specialized playthings, there are chains products specifically made for water play, consisting of cuffs that come furnished with suction mugs to stick to the surface area of your shower or bathtub. There are additionally knee pads that make the surface area of the bathtub much easier to stoop on in addition to vibrators furnished with suction mugs to hold up versus wall surfaces.

You'll require the devices to attain that if the suggestion of splashing water on your companion charms to you. For numerous, a showerhead with a hand-held part functions rather well. It'll permit you both to select the ideal strength for your play if the hand-held showerhead has flexible rate as well as water degrees.

Whatever kind of things you select, ensure to enable your chains equipment to totally completely dry after usage to stay clear of mold and mildew or corrosion

### Pick the Right Location

Water chains needs a lot more time, perseverance, and also hunting to guarantee you have a risk-free and also correct place contrasted to selecting a marine area for sex.

Make certain that you've adhered to the security suggestions over to guarantee that your house shower room is all set for kinky (as well as risk-free) water chains enjoyable. Pick a time when you're house alone or have outright personal privacy. Make certain that you have not drained pipes the warm water supply if you intend on a lengthy play session.

Swimming pools can be a truly enjoyable method to delight in water chains. If you pick to attempt as well as use a public swimming pool, make certain that you're doing this at a time where the swimming pool is shut to various other site visitors. If your feet can not touch the base, it's not an excellent location for play.

Whatever your water place is, make certain the water is secure and also tidy for sexes. Likewise attempt to warm up the water to a comfy temperature level to stay clear of burns or icy arm or legs disrupting your play if feasible.

### Check-In Afterwards

For that factor, it's vital that the 2 of you have a brief conversation later playing to make certain it was something that you both delighted in. Rather, attempt mounting your idea in a favorable light such as stating, "I actually enjoyed it when you sprinkled my busts with water, yet when you sprinkled my face with water it made it tougher to concentrate as well as take a breath on obtaining off. Following time, can we concentrate on simply my busts since you made it really feel so good?"

Of program, make certain to delight in yourselves! Do not stress regarding it if it transforms out that water chains simply isn't something you're right into! You do not need to be switched on by every sex-related concept that's around

# DISCIPLINE IN BDSM

The interpretation of self-control is the usage of policies and also or penalty to regulate a person or customize's behavior. Technique, or penalty, is generally provided as an outcome of some guideline being damaged. Paddling is an usual aspect in sensual chains tales, however just how is paddling in the room relevant to a type of technique?

While it could not appear to fit with chains, technique is a kind of psychological restriction as well as can take several types. Technique calls for a particular quantity of training, self-constraint, obedience, desire to adhere to policies, and also approval of authority. Both companions have a duty to play in this, as well as it's not constantly simple.

Submissives or bases have to agree to do what they're informed, without doubt, when they're offered a command. Since they currently understand what's anticipated of them based on formerly developed assumptions as well as policies, they likewise have to be eager to adhere to implied commands.

Failure to show discipline and obedience results in consequences, often in the form of punishment. Discipline, from your perspective, means you're willing to cede and follow rules control of daily functions or actions to your partner. Only you can decide if you can maintain discipline even when the rest of your life gets crazy and you aren't sure if you have the time to devote to it.

## INSTANCES OF DISCIPLINE

Techni□ue can take a selection of kinds and also be as easy or as facility as you pick to

bargain for your details scenario. It can be sex-related, solution oriented, or a mix.

Mental bondage is the ability to assume a physical position and maintain it for a set amount of time or until released. This can also be applied to something as simple as maintaining a specific position during kinky play, such as a spanking.

Regulations are a type of techni□ue typically produced to support and also look after a base or to aid attain individual objectives or perhaps a feeling of empowerment. When to head to bed, what to put on, as well as exactly how to deal with other individuals in the BDSM neighborhood are instances of policies that could be implemented.

Protocol is a manner of behavior to follow in specific situations like calling your Dominant "Sir" or not speaking without permission. In the local BDSM community, some protocols are followed when you first meet.

## Repercussions and also Punishment

E□ually as with anything in BDSM, self-control as well as just how it will certainly operate in your partnership needs to be

If a possible conse□uence is a hard limit for you, it must be respected. Conse□uences for disobeying a top vary from person to person.

Some instances consist of:

- Kneeling in the edge;

- Having your mouth rinsed with soap;

- Not talking with each other for a collection □uantity of time;

- Removal of benefits;

- Spankings - for those that do not delight in discomfort; or

- Lack of paddlings - for those that do delight in it.;

The idea is that the rules will be followed to avoid the consequences or that one taste of a punishment will keep someone from breaking the rules in the future. It's not unlike parenting, except that as an adult, you may be able to enjoy some kinky sex or a glass of wine after dealing with the conse□uences.

The means you have fun with chains or technique will certainly look various than the following kinkster, which's fine. If you just such as manacles or asking approval for climaxes throughout sex as well as nothing else time, you're equally as much right into chains as well as self-control as a person that will certainly invest hrs connecting complex knots as well as needing their companion to ask consent to make use of the washroom. The degrees of play might differ, however as long as you have the complete permission of your companion, absolutely nothing else issues.


## WHAT IS DOMINATION & SUBMISSION?

The huge D in BDSM means Dominance, among the core facets of kinky play

As you could have presumed, somebody that recognizes as a sex-related leading-- described as a Dom with a resources D in vernacular-- suches as to be the boss in the room.

The S represents Submission, as well as unsurprisingly still, these people like to be on the getting end of supremacy. Some submissives-- likewise called "belows" for brief-- merely like a companion that delights in getting on leading or connecting their hands to the bedposts.

Others require something extra severe to leave, like taking part in breath play or being curved over and also spanked. Dominants can be equally as large in their play choices, as well as their preferred sex acts can vary from making use of a sex plaything on their companion while they wince in thrilled climax, or snugly cuffing their ankle joints as well as wrists as well as screwing them silly.

Regardless of just how leading and also passive companions pick to play, permission as well as appropriate interaction underscore every little thing that takes place from the minute both individuals choose that their play session, typically called a "scene", starts. The secret is to just participate in BDSM have fun with a companion you can rely on as well as really feel comfy interaction specifically just how you really feel.

### Dominant

The very first time I ever before discovered myself in a bed room, bordered by rope and also in the existence of an eager woman, I will certainly admit I allow the minute go to my head. We invested extremely little time chatting regarding assumptions and also scenes, and also lots of time obtaining warm as well as troubled by the possibility of playing master as well as servant.

It took all of 5 mins of looking right into what must have been an enjoyable scene prior to she obtained a level appearance on her face, □uit wriggling and also type of sighed. Get rid of with clumsiness, we simply rested there, she limited by some lovely horrible knots, as well as me really feeling like the jerk in the space since I had not □uit to ask her what she desired. It finished up damaging the partnership, all due to the fact that no one assumed to talk up; we simply laughed as well as flushed as well as released right into something much past what our psychological understanding can deal with.

### Interaction.

Among the "catches" related to being the leading in a connection (which comes to be a typical challenge with a newbie Dom) is positioning much way too much focus on assumptions and also dreams, without quiting to get in touch with or give and even take notice of the various other individual. We believe "Dominant" as well as right away daydream regarding power and also control as well as working out those needs, without recognizing the truth: we are not the only individual below, we are not a real master or abductor or whatever, yet in some way that can obtain shed and also we presume that "Dominant" suggests simply that, and also the various other individual is simply an exchangeable prop that we are having fun with. As well as after that, to make issues worse, we have the possible to obtain mad when stated individual voices an argument - in this instance a completely affordable, nay, vital motion - as well as we respond.

## DEVELOPING BOUNDARIES & NEGOTIATION

For much of these sort of lists, you can suggest which acts are of rate of interest to you. Both companions ought to fill up these out-- it's not simply regarding what the passive is ready to involve in, the leading additionally have to really feel comfy executing these acts! If a below shares the wish to obtain put in the face, however the Dom really feels anxious or uneasy doing so, after that it's simply similarly crucial that (s) he suggest that (s) he has no need for slapping.

When experiencing these various items/acts, it's handy to suggest:

Points you absolutely wish to attempt

Points you have an interest in attempting however might require even more time (i.e. extra research study re uired, not prepared to try right now, etc).

Points you are tentative concerning, yet agree to attempt if your companion reveals a rate of interest in.

Points you do not truly wish to participate in, however are flexible (soft restriction).

Points that you absolutely do not intend to attempt ever before (tough limitation).

These are all vital points to take into consideration! You ought to do a "test-trial" of such tasks to obtain a great suggestion of what your companion can manage and/or is looking for. Offer your companion a couple of spanks on the butt and also obtain their responses, i.e.: "Harder", "Softer", "More", "Less", and so on

If this is your very first time "playing" (establishing out a Dom/sub dynamic in the bed room), it's great to straight-out develop the borders for that initial "scene"-

- i.e., although you both might have shown a passion in choking, probably you do not intend to begin with that said on your very first time-- begin gradually, there will certainly be a lot of time to experiment as well as check out all type of various points in the future!

Constantly regard well established borders-- even if points are going remarkable, as well as you assume s( he) would certainly be alright with going additionally, please do not (unless they offer you spoken authorization throughout the play session). Bear in mind, it's constantly much better for your companion to ask you to take points better in the future, than for you to take points as well much without authorization and also mess up the experience as well as make him/her unwilling to intend to attempt once again in the future.

Create a safeword. Constantly. Even if you do not believe you require one ... dreams are one point, real implementation of them is one more, your companion might not in fact appreciate the fact of an especially Dom/sub play as soon as (s) he experiences it so constantly play secure than be sorry.

One of the most usual safeword system is the "green-yellow-red" light system:.

" Green": Everything is going fantastic, maintain going!

" Yellow": Starting to really feel anxious/worried/hesitant, please take care and also sign in with me.

" Red": STOP NOW!


In cases in which you might not have the ability to utilize a safeword (i.e. gagging, breath play, having your face pushed right into a cushion, face-fucking, and so on), you will certainly re□uire to develop a "risk-free motion"-- it can be anything like blinking one eye a particular variety of times, touching your companion's wrist a specific variety of times, standing up a specific variety of fingers for your companion to see, breaking your fingers, whatever.

One more point in relation to safety and security is if you are ever before taking part in anything possibly high-risk-- i.e. breath play (consisting of light choking), blade play, effect play, chains, and so on-- please do your study (get in touch with on the internet sources, publications, overviews, BDSM neighborhoods, etc) so you understand exactly how to participate in these acts securely and also sensibly!

Continuously be mindful of on your own and also your companion throughout your play sessions. Or if you simply desire to do a fast check in, ask for a shade (thinking you are making use of the "green-yellow-red" light system). You can still inspect in with your companion without damaging the Dom/sub dynamic: You can ask them inquiries while still involving in the Dom duty: "I assume you be worthy of to be penalized, you're going to obtain 10 spanks to your limited little butt.

If you have any type of uncertainty in your mind, simply quit. Please, please DO NOT proceed, also if (s) he states (s) he is fine to obtain back right into it. As well as please mOTIVATE and also comfort her/him to utilize the safeword.


## Aftercare & "Debriefing".

Please take treatment of your companion after! Make certain she/he is literally fine, obtain them water if they require, examine for any kind of markings/bruises/cuts that might call for any type of treatment if suitable, and so on

.-- they might require favorable confidence that their companion took pleasure in being controlled as well as motivation that it was a satisfying experience.

An additional point that is excellent to do (specifically if you're simply beginning out) is to go over exactly how the session went-- talk concerning points that you both delighted in, ask what points you did not such as, and so on. Keep in mind, great as well as open interaction is one of the MOST necessary facets when integrating Dom/sub play in the room!


Due to the fact that this is just a novice's overview implied for those that are simply beginning out or are interested in a light domination-submission vibrant to include to their bed room play, I'm not going to dive right into anything actually BDSM-intensive (i.e. flogging/whipping, severe breath control, blade play, blood play, and so on).

A crucial facet to take into consideration is that a great deal of times "controling" does not simply imply having "rougher" sex, a great deal of the time it's regarding the mindset you covey, the words you claim, the appearance you offer-- a company grasp on the wrists as well as placing it over a companion's head while you grumble something mischievous in their ear might be extra reliable than merely hostile PIV fucking. You do not re□uire to be much h2er as well as larger to control a companion either. Maintain this in mind-- it's everything about the vibrant!

An additional part of this overview will certainly consist of some suggestions/examples of "unclean talk" throughout the overview of points you can state while participating in a controling act (they will certainly be included □uotes). A great deal of instances might consist of terms like "slut/whore/slave"-- please note that these terms can have EXTREMELY adverse responses and also be an instant turn-off for several ladies. Please replace them with even more favorable terms if that is what your companion chooses (i.e. "great girl/pet/slave", "sweetie", "angel", "infant woman")-- for even more in-depth ideas, seek advice from the "Erotic Verbal Degradation" versus "Praise/Compliments" areas.

Furthermore, however this overview was composed with the point of view of a male controling his women companion, so I excuse the restricted viewpoint of male Dom/female below heterosexual connection. The recommendations in this particular overview are purely from "what the Dom can do" point of view; there will certainly be a different overview for pointers on "what the below can do.".

This overview is NOT an assured group pleaser, please do not presume that you can simply comply with the actions and also your companion is going to like it-- I can ensure that there will certainly be visitors that will certainly dislike what is created right here or locate the dirty-talking outrageous as well as ridiculous. Once again this will certainly ALWAYS differ from companion to companion.




### Mild" Dominating

You can likewise push/pin her versus whatever tough surface area with her back encountering you as well as her front pushed versus the wall/floor/table/ desk/bed) and also play with her from behind. Hold down her wrists with a company grasp (over her head, behind her back, down by her sides). Lean your body weight versus her to produce the sensation like you are controling her body.

Place your hands all over her as if you can't get enough. Grab her breasts, s□ueeze her ass, cup her crotch. Worship her body with a kind of "animalistic" raw need.

Grab her chin or the back of her neck, and pull her mouth to yours. Try biting gently/nibble on her bottom lip or tongue.

Run your fingers with her hair as well as draw carefully. Yank her hair to make sure that it compels her to search for at you, provide her an attractive laugh, and also kiss her approximately. Tug her hair so it tilts/turns her head to the side to allow you to suck/kiss/nibble along her neck/shoulder blades/collarbones.

Idea: Grabbing smidgens of hair makes hair-pilling extra uncomfortable, bigger pieces much less so. Plucking the base of the hair is likewise much less uncomfortable than plucking completions.

Grind your hips against her crotch or between her ass cheeks (if you have her front pressed against something and her back facing you), let her feel your arousal pressed against her. "God I need/want to be inside of you."

Grab the sides of her pants (or belt holes if her pants permit) and pull her against your crotch so you can grip her ass. Rub her crotch through her pants/panties. Slide your hand down her pants (or up her skirt/dress) and slip a finger( s) through her panties and give her a slow fingering.

Taking it Further

Scraping: Use your finger nails as well as scrape along her back/shoulders/breasts/ belly. Or gently dig your nails right into her ass/back/legs.

Attacking: Bite along her neck/shoulder blades/collarbones/inner upper legs. Alternative with light kisses or tongue flicks. Attack her nipple areas, alternative with licking, swirling your tongue around the nipple area, as well as sucking.

Spanking: Slap her ass.

Squeezing: Give her nipple areas a fast pinch with your fingers. Alternative with mild licking/sucking/kissing, as well as attacking. Provide her ass/breasts/sides a fast painful capture as you have fun with her body.

Alternative in between discomfort as well as enjoyment: Whether you're damaging, attacking, paddling, or pinching, attempt rotating with mild acts (i.e. kissing, sucking/licking, touching) on that particular very same body component that you've brought upon discomfort on. The experiences as you move from providing discomfort as well as satisfaction can be actually exciting.

As with whatever, some women truly do not desire any type of noticeable body markings, so please maintain that in mind prior to you begin leaving hickeys, bite/scratch marks anywhere!

Individual fave is obtaining fucked with underwears on, after that having them taken off, and also pushed in my mouth as a trick] "You're/ My unclean little slut is being much as well loud, I'm going to have to discover a method to close that perfect/pretty little mouth of your own up."

Security factor: Because your mouth will certainly be gagged, you have to have a "risk-free motion" (or if you both create a developed "sound"-- i.e. her making a 'mmhpf' audio 3 times in sequence) as an indication to quit if points obtain excessive.

Make her plead. Make her ask some a lot more. "Good woman ..." Proceed to make her orgasm (with your tongue, fingers, dick, a plaything, whatever).

Obtain her to inform you when she's close/on the side if you can not inform when she is regarding to orgasm. When she informs you, quit your ministrations to make her plead, as well as provide it adequate time for her to "boil down" from the side, and afterwards start teasing her once more. Attempt to pay focus to nonverbal as well as spoken signs (i.e. modification in breathing price, body flush, grasping of sheets/you, various kinds of moaning/gasping/whimpering, and so on) when she's concerning to cum so you can begin obtaining a concept of when she's gotten to that factor for future referral.

After you've made her orgasm, "Have you had sufficient? ... I do not believe you have. Make her orgasm once again.

Suggestion: Using a sex plaything truly assists in this situation in case your tongue/fingers/penis burn out! Note: Some ladies end up being actually delicate after coming, as well as do not delight in any type of additional excitement after.

Make her satisfaction you: Force her on her knees as well as draw you off. "Suck me with that talented/pretty/perfect little mouth of your own.".

Make her preference herself: After you finger her, put your finger( s) in her mouth, as well as obtain her to cleanse them off. "You're such a horny little slut, you've almost drenched/coated my fingers/cock in your juices.

This is suitable if she's putting on a dress/skirt-- trek up her dress/skirt and also fuck her like that. If she has trousers, draw them off about. While fucking, take pleasure in searching her with her clothing-- move your hands up/down her t shirt to press her busts, slide your hands with her underwears to press her butt, and so on.

## POWER PLAY AND MORE EXPLICIT DOM/SUB DYNAMICS

Connect her wrists behind her back, as well as re□uire her to draw you off. Or connect her to the bed framework (ankle joints as well as wrists spread-eagle, or simply wrists) as well as tease her (excellent situation to integrate climax denial/forced climaxes right here!). "I'm going to tease you up until you plead me to allow you cum/for my dick."

If you wish to lengthen the bound experience or develop some good sex-related tension/anticipation, leave her bound so she can see you, and afterwards jack on your own off while delighting in the sight. "I assume I'm simply mosting likely to appreciate the sight for some time." Or alternative masturbating on your own and also moving your dick backwards and forwards her genital lips and also along her clitoris.

Security factor: NEVER leave somebody connected up alone in a space (if you require to leave to go to the washroom or anything like that for a couple of mins, make certain you can hear her if she calls out to you. NEVER LEAVE SOMEONE TIED aND ALSO gagged UP!).

Creating on her body: Use a dark pen (ideally one that does not smear as well very easy) and also create on a component (or different components) of her body./ my Master").

Make her place on a program for you: Command her to provide you a lap or an erotic dance dancing. Or obtain her to masturbate for you to view. Or select out a sex plaything (i.e. vibrator, vibe, rectal grains, and so on) for her to utilize on herself while you view her usage it.

As a whole, some pointers for unclean talk that MAY contribute to a power-play dynamic:

(Try integrating "currently" at the end of any of these commands in a strict voice).

Keep in mind: If your lady does not such as being coldly ordered around, you can include a "I desire you to ..." before these type of commands to make it perhaps much more satisfying or refined.

Producing a feeling of "property" or "possessiveness": "Mmm this tight/hot/sexy/ ideal little body/ass/pussy belongs to me. Also a simple: "Mine" or "You're mine" roared right into the ear might be really exciting.

Sexual Verbal Degradation [Caution: This is usually a hate it or like it severe, so please take care-- recognize your borders as well as recognize that these terms can have EXTREMELY adverse responses as well as be a prompt turn-off for lots of ladies]:

Call her a "dirty/filthy/naughty little slut/whore/cunt/ bitch/cumslut/sex plaything." "The only point you're excellent for is to be fucked/satisfying/serving me."

"You're my dirty/filthy/naughty little slut/whore/cunt/ bitch/cumslut/sex plaything. If she is reluctant, penalize her with a slap/spank/pinch. If you are not pleased with her feedback, penalize her up until she obtains it.

Make her call you "Sir" or "Master." Penalize her every single time she fails to remember to describe you as that.

Praise/Compliments [This is an excellent alongside those that are not right into spoken destruction, yet still appreciate the power-play (Master/slave) vibrant]:

Favorable terms like "Good girl/pet/slave" or "Sweetheart", "Angel", "Baby lady", "Little one."

You can "soften" "derogatory" terms by including a favorable adjective-- i.e. "What a sweet/good/beautiful/ sexy/perfect/lovely/ rather little slut/whore you are."

Or for taking her penalty so well: "You're such a great lady for taking your penalty so well."

## HOW TO MAKE YOUR SUB KEEP CRAWLING BACK

You desire to be the Dom that maintains the Subs creeping back huh? Allow's solve on that particular!

Point to take into consideration is that supremacy itself is not a details act however even more of a context on just how that act is used. That being claimed dominance can vary the whole range of whatever sex-related from cushion talk to points that can be taken into consideration torment in any type of various other context.

Before to We Begin

Prior to we obtain to much there are a couple of points to think about. You as well as your companion re□uirement to review these points as well as specify your convenience area. Taking points an action to much can lead to spoiling the entire point for your companion.

## Safewords. Utilize them!

Speaking of brakes, you may have heard of the term 'safeword' which is the word used to bring things to an immediate and complete stop. This however is not the only thing you should be aware of. Your partner needs to be comfortable using the safeword.

## Be Considerate, as well as Understand Your Partner's Needs!

Something that can not be worried sufficient is to think about that your companion is not the like all others. This is an overview not a guide definition you must utilize this as a way to seed concepts yet not as a detailed how-to. Some points on the mild checklist might be off restricts to you although some advanced or much more hostile points are terrific for you.

**Let's Get Started!**

*Sufficient of my rambling. You desire to obtain to the information?*

Kiss them like it's your means to take a breath. Order them by the chin, the sides of the face, or the rear of the neck as well as kiss them like your survival relies on it.

You can utilize it as a take care of to carefully guide after that in the instructions you desire to look. It might be at you, or you might also transform them around so you can obtain in behind them.

Search them like you are asserting what you are getting hold of. Lean in as you state and also do something like. Or probably something like "How are you permitted to have a butt this damn great?"

Also the flooring if absolutely nothing durable is close by. Whatever you select be certain to remember this is not an assault it's an expansion of you laying insurance claim to their body. This might confirm much more tough if you are women as well as your companion is male provided they will normally be more powerful than you.

Tease them a little bit by informing them they did this to you. If you have a favored component of their body you can claim "This is what looking at your ___ makes me desire to do."

Light damaging and also paddling is a great method to maintain the shock worth up. You are not out to cause discomfort or create damage, nevertheless with paddling you must not be worried to leave some short-lived marks. As □uickly as they are simply a little bit also kicked back SNATCH their focus with an additional swat.

Whether you are licking, attacking or drawing there are lots of points you can do to your companion's body and also several areas you can do it. Also if the area you pick that is not naturally sexually delicate attacking will certainly still have the very same result, simply bigger, as the damaging did earlier.

The preferred choice is to make them ask for it while you attract it out making certain when you do obtain to that climax it's a huge one with a large effect. The various other end of the range is to TELL your companion when they are going to orgasm. You may look like a fool if you inform your companion you are going to make them orgasm currently after that invested 2 mins functioning hard to make your declaration real.

If you are desiring something swift as well as fast, or you desire it to have the swift as well as fast sensation really feel complimentary to avoid some typical actions. If your companion is putting on some towels that provide you the choices of very easy accessibility such as a loosened suitable t-shirt, a skirt, loosened shorts or an outfit do not allow them being there obtain in your means. Also if your enjoyable takes 2 hrs leaving some fabrics on can make it really feel also much more rash and also warmed with simply a touch of that '☐uickie on the clothes dryer throughout the spin cycle' type of sensation.

Constantly maintain speaking. This is regarding maintaining your companion's mind involved. Not just does this maintain their mind in the video game yet it maintains them from being able to prepare for or anticipate what you will certainly do following enabling it to be a higher shock as well as have a higher impact.

If your companion is laying on their back stroll around so you are over their face and also inform them to those charming noises they are making to great usage. A great means of maintaining them involved can be to maintain them hectic also.

### Be a Bit More Frisky

Currently I expect you desire some extra hostile alternatives huh? I really feel obliged to attract your focus back to the safeword as well as various other comparable safety and security material on top. I will certainly presume you are a fairly liable grown-up so as opposed to stating it I'll simply reach the juicy little bits below!

Gagging by its actual nature it's an incapacitating act that is taking away your companion's capability to interact. If you take this course you will certainly require to have a different signal in area putting a higher demand on you to pay focus.

You might begin with manacles to bind their hands restricting their control as well as making them less complicated to route. Or take it additionally by linking each of their feet and also hands to a different bedpost spreading them out entirely. Whatever your selection is make certain they can constantly connect with you.

While it might be appealing to take a hostile position with your derogatory talk it's excellent to keep in mind there is the choice of applauding them for their acts. While it might be thought about a buying when taken out of context your companion might react far better to the derogatory appreciation than the derogatory disrespects.

### *Up Another Notch*

If you had you would certainly not have actually made it this much neither would certainly you still be reviewing. I'll inform you what, considering that you are such a great sporting activity as well as you made it this much allow's take it up a notch and also make it a bit much more intriguing.

While they have the particular objective of making you cum with their mouth maintain them from doing so as well quickly. A lot like stated over where you attract out your companion's orgasm you can do the exact same to on your own in this method by disturbing your companion's initiatives. Maintain them concentrated a lot more on you than the job at hand ... err mouth.

Whether it's their tummy, their back, their butt, their busts or their face; when you cum on them make certain you inform them what you are laying insurance claim to. When you do this make certain they understand it's not regarding preventing danger of maternity yet rather it's regarding you noting your area. When you are done, make certain they utilize their tongue to cleanse you up perfectly.

Devices as well as sex playthings is a topic of close to limitless conversation. A whole publication could be created on this component alone so I'll save the both people that. Make certain to consider your choices right here whether you are opting for vibes, grains as well as vibrators or ropes, tricks, blindfolds and also manacles for your chains play and even simply paddles, whips, belts as well as kitchen area spoons for paddlings.

Make them recognize each command you provide. You might also take it an action or 2 more by making them refer to you by a title such as Master or Mistress as well as thanking you for the command.

Provide them a collar; inform them they do not obtain to have undergarments any longer or simply make them just go nude for the remainder of the day. Make-up, fabrics and also hair are all points you can make them transform for you. If you have actually chosen to have actually dressed or partly fabrics sex you can also require them to put on the dirtied clothes for the rest of the day so they can scent and also really feel what occurred also hrs after it's over.

Paddling is one more point that can be intensified by consisting of added locations such as upper legs, busts, as well as also the face. Utilizing paddles or whips to the breast or face is fre□uently sufficient extra harmful than this warranted by the material of this overview.

Early on it was recommended that you can pin your companion and also pin their arms. Be really cautious at this time as it can be a great line in between lively battle as well as a journey to the medical facility if you have a companion that is specifically little.

Be certain to just press from the sides as well as in brief ruptureds. If your companion's resistance starts to go away or they are no much longer strained after that there is an excellent possibility you have actually currently taken it as well much. Be certain to provide your companion at the very least a couple of excellent breaths to recoup in between rounds of this.

A bite mark, a hickey, or something short-lived as well as else comparable. Simply make a mindful initiative to maintain such marks out of locations where they will certainly be seen throughout your companion's life outside of the bed room.

As a lot of ladies recognize, and also as specified even more than as soon as in this overview, dominance is as much concerning the state of mind as the activity. If you are doing well he will certainly follow your commands and also he will certainly appreciate you a whole lot a lot more both in the room and also out of it than if you feel you have to defeat on him to obtain what you desire out of him

## AFTERCARE IS REALLY IMPORTANT

After a session has actually come to an end no matter of exactly how or why it finished you ought to invest some time with your companion. It's additionally a great time to obtain some comments on just how to make certain following time about is simply a little bit much better. Following time around include even more of the previous and also go down some of the last.

# GUIDE TO SUBMISSION

A passive is a person that voluntarily gives up control to one more individual, normally to please a sexuality. If you're below reading this, opportunities are the idea of giving up control to one more individual has actually stimulated your rate of interest or has actually also obtained your sex-related juices streaming, in a manner of speaking. Believe you're strange?

Much from it, actually. Coming to be sexually passive is one of the most usual sex-related dreams.

5-10% of Americans takes part in sadism/masochism (S/M) methods for sex-related enjoyment at the very least periodically.

12% of females as well as 22% of males reported sensual feedback to an S/M tale.

55% of ladies and also 50% of males reported having reacted erotically to being attacked.

14% of guys and also 11% of females have actually had some sex-related experience with sadomasochism.

11% of guys and also 17% of females reported attempting chains.

Plainly, for lots of individuals, the dream of being purchased around, spanked as well as usually persuaded to execute sex-related acts can appear thrilling. And also if you desire to be a passive, what do you truly re□uire to recognize?


### *Inform Yourself*

Ending up being a passive is not a choice that ought to be made gently. Prior to you choose to start and also placed on your own at the grace of an additional, enlighten on your own on all points entry.

Some superb publications have actually been composed on the topic of entry and also supremacy, simply like this publication you are presently reviewing.

One more means to find out more regarding what it's like to end up being a passive is to go to a "munch". A "munch" (brief for "hamburger munch") is a laid-back celebration for people thinking about the dominant/submissive way of living. Participating in these celebrations is a wonderful means to get in touch with knowledgeable people as well as find out more concerning the way of living.

***If You're Really the Submissive Type, figure out***

Not remarkably, passive habits generally comes really normally to real submissives. Just how can you inform if you're a real passive?

Typically, real submissives have a need to please a much more leading individual and also might also be transformed on by the idea of being embarrassed or subdued. On the flip side, nonetheless, if sending to one more individual transforms you off, being a passive most likely isn't for you.

Ask on your own truthfully why you desire to end up being a passive. Never ever come to be a passive if you really feel that you're being pushed right into it.

***Identify Your Level of Submission***

There are a couple of various uni□ue degrees of prominence as well as entry. Some individuals, as an example, merely utilize prominence as well as entry to include a little flavor to their sex lives. This generally consists of dream role-playing in the bed room once in a while, with some light paddling, filthy talk or chains

Part-time submissives locate that the passive way of living is a far more fundamental part of their lives. They might change right into a passive throughout specific times, such as throughout sex or when checking out a BDSM club. They will certainly frequently buy clothing as well as various other props, yet will not generally allow their function hinder various other locations of their lives.

Full time submissives, on the various other hand, are typically the determined gamers in the BDSM video game. These kinds of submissives might also be looking to live in a full time dominant/submissive partnership.

Just like all points in life, when it concerns supremacy as well as entry, it's generally best to begin little as well as function your means up. Perhaps attempt a little dream role-playing prior to you totally send to a permanent leading.

### Know Your Limits

Does the idea of being caned make you desire to shrink in the edge? Simply simply due to the fact that others delight in something does not indicate that you have to. Know your restrictions and also stand company!

### Connect

While interaction is necessary in any type of partnership, it's definitely vital in a dominant/submissive partnership. Currently's not the moment to be timid; if you're unpleasant with the idea of sharing your innermost libidos and also turn-offs it can actually impact your security - in addition to whether you appreciate your experiences. As a passive, you have to be able and also ready to honestly interact with your companion or companions to guarantee that all sex play is genuinely consensual.

Prior to a scene or connection starts, you and also your companions must share your desires, wishes, and also sex-related dreams. It is similarly crucial to make your companions conscious of any kind of limitations as well as turn-offs you might have. Make your limitations understood as well as established borders immediately.


### Place Safety

Recently, the term "secure, consensual and also rational" has actually come to be something of an adage for the BDSM neighborhood as well as BDSM play. If you're considering BDSM bet the very first time, or perhaps if you're a hard expert, safety and security needs to be a No. 1 concern.

Constantly take the time to find out just how to effectively as well as securely utilize any type of props as well as playthings, as well as constantly develop a safeword prior to starting any kind of BDSM play.

This basic word or expression can be talked by a passive at any kind of time they desire to reduce down or ☐uit a scene, no inquiries asked.

### *Distinguish Fantasy from Reality*

It's essential that you're able to differentiate dream from truth if you're ready to take that initial action right into a dominant/submissive partnership. Unless you have an additional plan, you and also your leading need to bear in mind that your role-playing is simply that - playing.

Do not allow your leading's activities as well as words reach you, as well as keep your pride. Keep in mind that unless you connect with your leading, he or she will just presume that you're pleased with exactly how your partnership is going. Obviously, if your companion does not appreciate you sufficient to ☐uit exceeding your limitations, regard on your own sufficient to finish the partnership.

### *Grow Patience*

Coming to be a real passive takes a wonderful offer of time and also persistence. Numerous submissives might also go with an official "training" duration, which can take months or also years.

As well as if you do choose to open this brand-new phase in your life, have a good time with it. You might select to shut it in the future, or it might end up being a huge part of that you are. In any case, discover what you can from the experience and also, most significantly, appreciate it!

## WHAT KIND OF SUBMISSIVE ARE YOU?

You assume you may be passive however after that you do some study as well as really feel that everything appears as well severe. You're not exactly sure what you are any longer, besides switched on and also puzzled.

Limiting the globe of D/s - especially entry - in a couple of brief paragraphs might appear difficult, yet never ever are afraid, I'm below to try simply that

### The Key Types of Submissives

If you believe you may be passive, inspect out the typical classifications provided below. For the document, not all submissives are masochistic, and also not all Dominants are sadists.

### *Bedroom-Only Submissive*

A bed room passive desires their companion to control them however just throughout sex-related affection. Bedroom-only submissives might want to develop a safeword to make use of with their companion if they start to really feel harmful or uneasy in any type of method.

### *24/7/365 Submissive*

Entry in this kind of partnership consists of sex-related entry, yet will certainly commonly likewise incorporate the efficiency of residential jobs, routines and also well established policies in between the passive as well as leading. What most outsiders see when they observe a pair in a 24/7 D/s connection is one companion that delays to the various other and also follows their lead, yet this does not imply that there isn't shared regard in between the Submissive as well as leading.

### *Pets & Furries*

Passive acts might include acting like a family pet by creeping on all fours or making animal audios. Dominants might provide their submissives pet-related presents such as a chain, food recipe as well as squeaky playthings. There are also distinct, tail-shaped rectal plugs that submissives might want to put on.

### Littles & Babygirls

This is one of the most misinterpreted categories of passive. Littles and also babygirls are 2 different courses of passive, although they have some features in typical.

### Servant

When servants go into a connection, normally referred to as a Master/slave partnership, they commonly provide up all legal rights within their partnership. All information are connected, worked out, and also concurred upon prior to the partnership starts.

### Solution Submissive

A solution passive is distinctly non-sexual. Solution submissives frequently do residential responsibilities such as cleansing as well as food preparation, however might likewise manage various other work as well as jobs as set by both companions. This passive is fre☐uently part of a bigger polyamorous D/s partnership or house.

There are no rapid as well as difficult policies for being a passive. The points that matter most in a BDSM connection are excellent interaction, arrangement, trust fund and also security.

## How to Ask Your Partner to Be Your Dominant

After months of analysis, exploring, tracking the web as well as assuming, you're favorable you're a passive. When you look at your companion, you think they might be your Dominant. Exactly how do you chat to them regarding it?

He was as well as giggled in shock, as well as a little unpleasant, however he was likewise prepared to pay attention. Which, at the end of the day, is all you truly re□uire.

This is not a magic repair for your partnership.

" I believed he would certainly be delighted when I stated it, and also I assume he was eliminated, however inevitably, it still could not repair or conserve our marital relationship," Peep claimed.

BDSM isn't a magic tablet, however it's still vital to be real to on your own as well as interact your demands with your companion.

### Just how to Approach Your Partner

When you chat to your companion, the actions I make use of to chat to my companion regarding including brand-new twists or changing our dynamic aren't that a lot various than what you need to think about.

• Let them understand you re□uire to speak, and also select a great time.

• Analyze what you wish to state.

• Do not wait as well long, specifically if your re□uirements aren't being satisfied.

• Take the discussion gradually.

• Speak about what you are really feeling as well as assuming.

• Aim your companion to sources to read more.

• Mention the kinky sex (which could be a marketing indicate your companion), however speak about the various other aspects of D/s that talk to you.

• Recognize that they might require time to recognize what this suggests, take care of any kind of false impressions they have, as well as discover more prior to they concur.

• Be all set to transform on your own.

• Maintain Your Expectations Realistic

• Believe concerning it for a 2nd. Neither will certainly your companion.

As soon as you're out, exactly how to make it function?

"D/s needs dedication from both of you," Peep claimed.

" Your companion will not be the Dominant of your desires. Keep in mind, you're not the only one in the partnership," Caitlyn described.

DD concurred. "I truly assumed I was mosting likely to create the manuscript, maintain control, and also state exactly how my spouse was mosting likely to carry out. I was so incorrect," DD stated.

As a passive, you will certainly have to con□uer years of being in control, not allowing go, and/or not completely trusting your companion to deal with problems. You might transform even more than your companion.

### What Happens After the First Conversation.

Prior to you leap up from the table or sofa or any place you have this discussion to obtain kinky, reduce down for a min. If you're both ready as well as prepared for warm, kinky, ape sex, go for it.

Share the sources you located to discover concerning D/s. I have not fulfilled a kinkster yet that's not eager to aid out somebody that's attempting to find out much more.

" Keep chatting and also discover coaches," Peep claimed.

### You both still have plenty to find out.

DD uses recommendations based upon her very own distinct experience as well as challenging roadway to entry. "It begins with your entry and also regard of your companion," she stated. "Acknowledge the count on concerns as well as place your entry right into activity.".

Be prepared to chat and also maintain speaking. Your companion never ever has actually been and also never ever will certainly be a mind visitor. With any luck, your companion is ready to take the trip with you.


## Switching During BDSM

Not everybody really feels attracted to just one group of BDSM identification. Numerous lifestylers switch over backward and forward in between passive and also leading duties, therefore the fundamental term "button".

For virginal twist pairs, companions will certainly switch room functions relying on the day of the week, exactly how they're really feeling presently, or in some cases all within a solitary round of sex. For polyamorous pairs or those within open connections, buttons may take pleasure in acting out various BDSM functions with various companions based upon their private sex-related chemistry as well as choices.

# What is Sadism & Masochism?

Currently right here's where you may presume points obtain terrifying, yet once more, bear in mind that absolutely nothing negative can take place when you have fun with a companion that pays attention to your requirements and also respect your wellness.

## Sadism and Masochism

Whether you call it sadism as well as masochism, sadomasochism, or S&M (I'm considering you, Rihanna), this branch of BDSM is potentially one of the most misinterpreted component. Regarded a psychological illness by Sigmund Freud in 1905 with its name originated from the Marquis de Sade, a male relatively withdrawn in approval, sadomasochism can be one of the most fierce of all BDSM tasks and also is stuffed with one of the most threat.

## What Is S&M?

The sadist delights in offering discomfort, while the masochist delights in getting it. In contrast to preferred idea, not all sadomasochism play ends in sex -also though it's a turn-on for the gamers -neither is it a "demand" in D/s partnerships.

If you're a sadist, you may take pleasure in dishing out discomfort, destruction, anything, or embarrassment to trigger the suffering of your ready as well as consenting masochist. As a masochist, you may delight in really feeling physical discomfort, being embarrassed, or just experiencing for your top or Dominant.

## Various Types of Play

As I stated previously, sadomasochism can entail psychological or physical discomfort. The physical is most usual as well as varies along a large range of tasks:

• Nipple area and also clitoral clamps;

• Penis as well as round torment;

• Wax play;

• Blade play, which might or might not include blood being attracted;

• Chains in order to create discomfort. The busts are bound securely, creating blood to swimming pool.

• Re□uired Orgasms: -one climax behaves, 2 are much better, yet several climaxes from delicate genitalia can be excruciating; or

• Paddlings: -for some in the BDSM way of life, paddlings are an aspect of penalty as well as techni□ue for negative habits, however in sadomasochism, they offer an additional function completely.

If it creates discomfort, as well as you as well as your companion appreciate it, you can include it to the physical sadomasochist column, even if you do not locate it on typical listings.

On the various other side of points, embarrassment as well as destruction are a type of psychological S&M play. Various other kinds consist of pleading, being dealt with like a pet or item of furnishings, slapping of the face, kissing or licking feet, as well as a lot, a lot a lot more.

## AUTHORIZATION AND ALSO SAFETY

What divides the sadist from an abuser that belongs in prison is one word: approval. Like all components of BDSM, complete interaction as well as disclosure are a demand for secure S&M play.

For those brand-new to S&M, no task ought to start without some anticipation or training. If you've never

ever utilized a flogger, your companion's base or back are not the initial location to attempt it out. Consult with regional individuals in the way of life at a BDSM club, enjoy video clips on-line, and also method on a cushion prior to you ever before attempt something out on an individual.

Accountable sadists in the BDSM way of living recognize the relevance of permission and also do not take part in any kind of task without it. Masochists have an obligation to yield their worries and/or case history to ensure that they are not accidentally hurt by the psychological or physical discomfort that's being brought upon. Somebody with previous misuse that finds themselves caused in specific scenarios will certainly require to reveal that to make sure that their top does not take part in anything that might cause an episode.

It's excellent for anybody in BDSM, however particularly masochists as well as sadists, to end up being accredited in emergency treatment and also CPR. Despite having outstanding prep work, a lot of interaction, as well as considerable understanding, points can and also do fail throughout play or a scene. Understanding what to do in an emergency situation can conserve an individual's life.

Marks and also contusions are a badge of honor for several masochists and also harsh, physical play fre☐uently ends up being loud as well as appears mad, do not believe your authorization will certainly be approved in a neighborhood court room or by the authorities. Play clever and also risk-free.

Similar to any other part of BDSM, the degree of pain or discomfort brought upon is pre-determined by both the Dom as well as below prior to the real play starts. Lighter types of masochism as well as sadism can include tickling, making use of a vibe to tease your companion while they're bound, or gently damaging them with your nails. A lot more severe types can entail extreme pleasing up until your companion asks you to ☐uit, transform the vibe approximately its greatest setup and also 'requiring' your companion to climax up until fatigue, or damaging your companions back up until you injure.

Since BDSM play can include greater than simply the typical sex-related physical liquids traded in between genital areas-- like blood, pee, or rectal mucous-- it's critical that every person entailed obtains normal STD examinations as well as divulges their examination results with every companion. The only people that can escape a one-off browse through to the medical professional are totally virginal pairs that continue to be sincere as well as dedicated to their companions.

For those of us that appreciate it, sadism as well as masochism enhances sex-related satisfaction. Understand, however, simply since we such as kinky discomfort does not suggest we appreciate various other kinds of discomfort. It's not the exact same kind of discomfort at all.

" Hurt me, harm me!" sobs the masochist.

The sadist responds, "No.".

I recognize of no far better summary of sadism as well as masochism than that.


## SSC vs. RACK

Authorization as well as interaction are the 2 most essential aspects in BDSM. Individuals in the BDSM way of living have various techni☐ues of categorizing whether a task is aLRIGHT and also secure to do. Choosing which concept to comply with is an individual choice, - as is whatever in BDSM, - however it assists to have a standard understanding of each.

### Safe, Sane, as well as Consensual

Maintain it secure. Do not make use of a flogger for the very first time on an individual; - utilize a cushion up until you obtain made use of to the activities as well as the sensation. Oh, and also method, method, method prior to you attempt it on your companion.

Be practical in the tasks you select. Do not do something that has an actual threat of injury unless both of you are an educated in just how to do it as well as understand exactly how to take care of emergency situations.

Maintain it consensual. Whether it's by utilizing a secure word or connecting difficult restrictions and also borders, do not do anything without the complete approval of your companion. When in uncertainty, ask as well as quit.

### Danger Aware, Consensual Kink

SHELF is utilized most usually by those that stress that SSC is wide as well as well obscure. Blade play holds the threat of blood being attracted. Prior to you attempt it, you require to recognize the actual dangers.

Consensual. There's that word once more - consensual. If you can not respond to these concerns, it may not be consensual.

Below's the method to recognize if you re□uire RACK. If the solution is indeed, after that you re□uire RACK.

Neither SSC or RACK are ideal and also consist of every solitary feasible variant or circumstance. Do not attempt a brand-new task with your companion till you've investigated it, discovered regarding it, asked concerns, and also exercised on a non-living item, if feasible. Whichever you choose, SSC or RACK, follow them, utilize them, as well as be clever regarding your kinky tasks.

# THE IMPORTANCE OF COMMUNICATION

Interaction is the solitary essential element in BDSM. If you're just right into paddlings by complete strangers or you're in a 24/7 Master/slave connection, I do not care. Absolutely nothing in BDSM must ever before take place without lots of interaction.

## WHAT DOES COMMUNICATION LOOK AND ALSO SOUND LIKE?

" I truly do not like it when you touch me there."

" I'm not thinking about [fill in the empty with your most disliked task or fetish]".

" I liked it when you kissed my neck, however when you attacked me. It harmed, as well as I really did not like it.".

" I'm sensitive to latex.".

" I have bronchial asthma.".

The viewpoint that you re□uire to inform your companion every little thing isn't simply buzz. This isn't practically constructing a solid connection or discovering the love of your life (although both are definitely results of great interaction). Speaking out as well as sharing information regarding on your own, your sort, your disapproval, what you believe, and also your health and wellness effect your experience in BDSM.

If you're believing that some information are merely as well individual to share, bear in mind that he or she will certainly more than likely see you entirely nude while you're salivating, sweating, wincing, as well as shouting. Just how much a lot more individual can you obtain than that?


## INTERACT YOUR NEEDS.

Both sides, lower and also leading, Dominant and also passive, have to have the ability to connect their.

A sadist re□uires to understand if the various other individual is a masochist. Prior to you connect somebody up with rope, you need to recognize if your companion has inade□uate flow or any kind of kind of stress and anxiety when they can not relocate openly.

BDSM is not a prejudiced occasion. 2 (or even more) individuals are included and also every one ought to have their demands fulfilled, yet no one can amazingly recognize what you require as well as what you desire.

Deposit your issue concerning harming your companion's sensations. As long as you deal with the various other with respect while you tell them what functioned or really did not, a fully grown individual will certainly have the ability to manage it. The only method for both individuals to appreciate what's occurring is to recognize what obtains you off - and also, when something brand-new is attempted, what does not.

## INTERACT YOUR BOUNDARIES.

There are simply some points individuals do not such as. I do not such as rough roadway ice lotion (I understand, some of you are wheezing in shock). That's a streamlined contrast, however if you've ever before been provided ice lotion as well as after that discovered out it had not been a taste you such as, you recognize the frustration.

Prior to I involve in BDSM tasks with a brand-new companion, I inform them. If I do not make it clear that I do not such as that kind of play, I could be in for a large shock at some factor - and also not locate it hot, sensual, or pleasing. That desires kinky sex or BDSM play that's unfulfilling?

The excellent point concerning interaction in BDSM, - particularly when you establish restrictions, - is that you can constantly go back later on and also transform your mind. If you're continually connecting with your companion, you can inform them that you've provided a previous difficult limitation, claim sphere tricks, even more assumed, and also you would certainly such as to attempt it.

## TRUST FUND AS WELL AS INTIMACY.

What does interaction obtain you aside from enjoyable as well as kinky BDSM play? It develops trust fund as well as affection in between you and also your companion. When you're talking with each other in a significant means concerning your desires, your demands, your needs, what functioned, what really did not function, and also your borders, you find out more concerning each other than you ever before believed feasible.

It brings you closer to that individual. Recognizing that they are connecting in the exact same means and also sharing the tiniest information of that they are brings you with each other.

For anybody brand-new to the BDSM way of living, you could be shocked to understand that bases and also.

submissives have even more control than you understand. A great Dominant or leading will certainly never ever breach a difficult restriction that has actually been connected to them. They additionally will not take part in brand-new tasks up until they've spoken with their base or passive concerning them, either.

Connecting limits and also difficult limitations is one element of the control a passive has; the various other is the usage of secure words. Make certain every person in the scene recognizes it. If a passive or base will certainly be incapable to vocally interact throughout a scene, a hand signal of some kind ought to be in area.

Safe words aid interact a sensation of threat, undesirable discomfort, or various other sensations as well as feelings that suggest the play or scene requires to instantly quit. If a risk-free word is made use of consistently in scenes and also various other play, you re□uire to speak to each various other regarding what the underlying issue might be whether it's a physical discomfort, a concern, a concern, or a tough limitation you really did not understand around.

One Final Thought on Communication.

If permission is the crucial to BDSM in basic, - after that interaction is the important very first action. No one is a mind viewers, and also you will just obtain out of BDSM what you place right into it. Just after that can you experience the complete elegance and also sexiness of BDSM.

## BDSM Dungeon

A BDSM dungeon is an interior room marked especially for BDSM play or BDSM scenes. Any kind of number of BDSM tasks can take place in a dungeon consisting of tasks such as flogging, chains, suspension, blood play, age play, and also resistance play.

The term dungeon does not always suggest that these areas remain in castles or underground. Personal dungeons, such as those inside personal houses, might inhabit room in cellars, however can likewise be established in rooms, extra spaces, and even big walkin storage rooms. Public dungeons might inhabit bars or storage facilities as well as are normally available to the general public, although they normally run extremely silently.

Sex clubs, dungeons-- they seem a little terrifying and also a great deal mystical. Prior to you assume a BDS M dungeon is a location you can not picture going, it might assist to recognize exactly how they function and also what goes on behind shut doors.

### Public vs. personal Dungeons

Be conscious that some dungeons are public and also others are exclusive. Public dungeons will certainly allow any individual in that adheres to specific standards, demands as well as guidelines.

Exclusive dungeons are commonly by invite just. My favored dungeon just enables individuals that have actually been directly vetted by the proprietor of the dungeon or pick pals. Since they do not exercise secure BDSM or since they are seen as killer, individuals are usually declined admission.

### Not Everyone Gets In

If a dungeon calls for ID, you're not going in without that, no matter of your age. Dungeons can and also do prohibit individuals for declining to adhere to the dungeon regulations as well.

Dungeons are commonly really mindful regarding that they allow in. One mistake with the regulation or one individual that does not regard safety and security or personal privacy, and also the entire dungeon might be closed down - or even worse.


### Anticipate to Pay a Cover

Dungeons are companies, and also they've obtained costs to pay. Room, electrical energy, team ... none of it comes cheap.

Subscriptions might be readily available for your regional dungeon. Make certain to ask what you obtain for your subscription cost prior to you sign up with.


### Understand Protocols

Procedures are extremely essential in numerous BDSM communications. A lot of dungeons will certainly either upload the regulations or clarify them on your very first go to.

There are, nonetheless, some "basic" methods that you'll see in several dungeons:

- Dominants can not touch submissives without consent from the passive's Dominant.

- Submissives have to utilize honorifics with all Dominants, not simply their very own. "Sir" as well as "Ma'am" prevail, yet ask if you're unclear.

- Dominants do not speak with an additional Dominant's passive without authorization.

There might be extra methods at your neighborhood dungeon. Some of the procedures will not use if you're a solitary passive. When unsure, ask.

### *Security Is Paramount*

Safe, consensual and also rational is a consistent refrain on the planet of BDSM. From the moment you stroll in the door and also reveal your ID till the moment you leave, your security as well as the safety and security of everybody else need to be leading of mind.

Dungeon screens can be located throughout a dungeon. They keep an eye on individuals that are playing to make certain safewords aren't neglected, poor method does not endanger somebody's wellness, and also that onlookers aren't obtaining in the method of the activity.

When to Ask Them, do not Be Afraid to Ask Questions-- But Know

Not every person that goes to a dungeon takes part in a scene or plays. Some individuals just go to hang out, mingle as well as observe.

Ask the dungeon display. Wait till the scene is done and also every person has their clothing back on if you desire to ask the individuals entailed.

### Nakedness Is the Norm however Not Necessary

The initial time I went to a regional dungeon, I saw extra boobs than I assumed feasible. Several individuals use their fetish e uipment to the dungeon-- or they transform after they get here.

Various other times, no one strips their garments off till they end up being included in a scene. The only point I put on throughout a scene is a band. Simply since nakedness is enabled as well as usual in dungeons does not suggest every person is obtaining nude.

### Not All Dungeons Allow Sex

One dungeon I go to does not permit infiltration or liquids. Every dungeon is various. Obtain a dungeon display instantly if they do not.).

As with anything else, when in question, ask. No one must make you really feel awkward since you do or do not obtain active throughout a scene.


### Examine Your Body and/or Kink Shame at the Door

When you stroll via the doors of a dungeon, specifically when the evening is in complete swing, you will certainly see points you never ever thought of. A person will most likely be totally nude-- and also they most likely will not have a cover girl's body.

The dungeon is a terrific area to see individuals from all strolls of life taking pleasure in any type of number of proclivities as well as twists. If you reveal disrespect to a person's body or scene, you might discover on your own looking at the club from the exterior ... by on your own.

In fact, a BDSM dungeon is a location for kinksters to obtain with each other, find out something brand-new, hang out and also have a little enjoyable. Simply maintain in mind that the dungeon can and also must be a secure location to be your kinky self also.

Keep in mind: There are 2 great methods to locate out regarding what dungeons are in your location: word of mouth as well as Fetlife. If you do not have any kind of neighborhood kinky good friends to inform you where to go, you'll desire to inspect Fetlife to locate a club or dungeon.

# YOUR FIRST BDSM PLAY PARTY

At this casual or official celebration, individuals match off right into teams as well as appreciate doing kinky points to one an additional while various other kinky individuals see. Generally done in an exclusive location that's shut to the public, it could appear difficult to get as well as locate entry to a kinky play event.

Going to a play event for the initial time can be terrifying. Discover whatever you require to recognize regarding going to a play celebration in the inquiries listed below.

## JUST HOW DO I FIND A PLAY PARTY?

The most convenient method to discover your regional play events are with your regional twist teams. While some individuals place on exclusive play celebrations in their houses, many play celebrations are placed on by twist teams in the location.

In the Internet age, it can be quite easy to locate out the closest BDSM teams to you. Attempt Fetlife, a kinkster social network, to discover some of the teams that are closest to you.

Relying on where you live, you might re□uire to be prepared to make a little a drive in order to locate a play event in the future. While even more kink-friendly locations like Los Angeles or New York might have normal play events taking place, if you're in a much less dynamic location, a 2 or 3 hr drive is reasonably typical.

Huge, team occasions will certainly enable nearly anybody to sign up as long as you pay the greater entry cost. These occasions usually have instructional programs together with the play celebrations. Smaller sized, more-private occasions might have various other re□uirements prior to you can go to, however these kinds of occasions are made for a solitary night of enjoyable.

## WHAT ARE THE REQUIREMENTS TO ATTEND A PLAY PARTY?

Every team has their very own play event demands. It's vital that you review or ask regarding the demands prior to trying to RSVP for a celebration if you're looking at going to a twist occasion for a regional team. Some typical demands consist of going to numerous munches, being vetted by a present participant, participating in a new member positioning, or being an energetic participant of one more reliable twist team.

The majority of teams will certainly need an RSVP to the event after you satisfy the various other re□uirements. Never ever reveal up to a play event unwelcome.

## WHAT ACTUALLY HAPPENS AT A PLAY PARTY?

In contrast to lots of people's ideas, play events generally aren't simply large sex orgies. Some play celebrations do not also permit complete nakedness or sex-related infiltration of any kind of kind. The task at a play event is absolutely concentrated on the kinky side of points, so anticipate to see a great deal of hot, fetish-fun points.

The kind of play event set up relies on whether you're going to a substantial occasion, a smaller sized occasion, or an exclusive play event, yet you can anticipate to see kinky furnishings (such as spanking benches or a St. Andrew's cross). Anticipate loud songs as well as individuals scantily as well as sexily worn kinky clothing. You must additionally anticipate to see individuals appreciating kinky scenes throughout the event such as paddlings, floggings, rope chains, electro-sex, and also much more.

If you're brand-new, you might be presented to some of the individuals in fee when you get here. There are hardly ever factors for a DM to obtain included as the secure word system maintains most play times well within what everybody would certainly take pleasure in.

At many play celebrations, any kind of kind of scene that is extremely visuals (such as points that consist of blood or physical li□uids) will most likely be cordoned off in one more location. Is specifically activating to you, alert the personnel of the play event in advance of time.

## WHEN SHOULD I SHOW UP? CAN I BE FASHIONABLY LATE?

In order to avoid disruptions as well as unexpected exploration of the celebration, lots of play events will certainly have the doors secured to any type of outdoors visitors after a specific quantity of time. The majority of event coordinators will certainly advertise this details with your RSVP, so make certain you can reveal up at the real begin time.

## What Should I Bring?

If you're transforming right into your kinky clothes at the event, bring your cosmetics as well as apparel with you. If you prepare on playing at the event, any type of kinds of restrictions or playthings must be in your bag. Do not fail to remember to bring your picture ID in order to obtain right into the event in the very first area.

Generally, bring standard kinky materials along with your ID as well as some cash money. To be on the risk-free side, you might wish to bring more secure sex products in case you satisfy a person at the event as well as intend to have a good time after that.

## What Shouldn't I Bring?

Make certain to examine the policies of the play event prior to trying to generate a mobile phone. Never ever, EVER effort to bring a cam unless it has actually been gotten rid of by the event proprietors. Some play events additionally ban alcohol (to make certain every person is of sound mind to grant all tasks), so inspect your play celebration policies prior to loading any kind of li□uor in your bags.

## Just how Should I Dress?

The outfit code for any kind of provided play event will certainly differ by the guidelines of the company as well as the event. As a guideline of thumb, the default presumption is to constantly clothe in ordinary, laid-back road garments to obtain right into the location.

When it comes to your sexier clothes, some play celebrations might have guidelines concerning what you should put on. Needing sexier clothing aids maintain the play celebration sensation like the sensuous fantasy-land that individuals will certainly appreciate.

The majority of play celebration invites will certainly have a clear listing of any type of kind of gown demands when you RSVP, yet if you're at a loss for what to use, in a pinch, normal underwear or simply a hot set of underclothing can operate as kinky wear. Simply do not go striking arbitrary individuals at the event. Use something that makes you really feel hot, yet bear in mind, if you intend on having fun, you might desire to load some footwear that enable you to conveniently stand as well as maintain your e□uilibrium.

Dipping into a play event can be an interesting experience! I extremely suggest you prevent playing this very first night as well as simply take pleasure in the experience if this is your initial play celebration. Take pleasure in that basic sensation of stimulation as you spend time while every one of various other scenes happen.

If you're ready to play, though, you need to understand that before every scene, there are negotiations. You will need to discuss what you are (and aren't) OK with during your scene. Mentioning you're new to kink and play parties is a great idea as it helps your play partner ease you into some of the pleasure.

With the invention of Fetlife and other kinky social networks, you can send a private message to people who are attending an upcoming play party. Be aware that this may not be met with much success unless you've become a familiar face at play parties; while some people will be willing to play with new people, you'll have a much higher success rate if you've been an active member of the community.

It's also possible to arrange a scene with someone while at the play party. Wait until the person seems unengaged in a scene or with another person, and feel free to go up and ask if they 'd be interested in doing a scene. Have a good idea of what you 'd like to do.

If the person you ask says no, don't take it personally. They may have come here with a monogamous partner or they may only play with people who have asked ahead of time. They may even have stage fright and may only be comfortable playing in public if they've had weeks to plan out their scene.


## Can I Talk at a Play Party? Can I Join In?

Talking at a play party is definitely encouraged, and just for that reason, many play parties have a "social area" that's away from the scenes. You can imagine how distracting it might be to listen to someone's recounting of their office fight while you're attempting to enjoy a sensual spanking, so speaking near scenes is frowned upon.

Stick to watching the scenes unless you've negotiated joining in before the scene starts. That said, if you watch a super-hot scene between people and now would like to play with someone from the scene, wait until the scene is over, give them some time to wind down, and then approach and ask about the possibility of playing with that person.

## Can I Take Photos at a Play Party?

Many people who attend play parties want to keep their identities secret. Make sure to respect the rules of the play party, and if you're unsure if it's allowed, always, always ask the party host.

## Should I Go to Another Play Party?

Some people find themselves uncomfortable after their first play party. Play parties can be a ton of fun, so don't give up after your first one.

# VOCABULARY OF **BDSM**

The vocabulary of BDSM can be daunting to newbies (newcummers, heh heh). Allow's begin with the essentials: "BDSM" stands for chains as well as entry, technique and also supremacy, as well as sadism and also masochism, the core columns of kinky enjoyable. Past that, there's an entire language to define the consensual power exchange techniques that take location under the BDSM umbrella.

## A IS FOR AFTERCARE

Aftercare is the method of monitoring in with one an additional after a scene (or "play session," a.k.a., the time in which the BDSM occurs) to make certain all celebrations really feel good and also cool concerning what simply went down. The leading companion might bring the passive ice for any kind of swellings, yet it's essential to recognize that aftercare includes psychological treatment as well as physical.

## B IS FOR BONDAGE

Chains is the act of linking each other up. The leading companion is limiting the passive utilizing ropes, manacles, Velcro, specialized hooks, holds, or merely a belt if you're on a budget plan.

**C IS FOR CBT (COCK AS WELL AS BALL TORTURE).**

In BDSM, CBT does not describe cognitive behavior modification, it describes "cock and also sphere torment," which is precisely what it seems like: The leading will certainly bind, whip, or utilize their high-ass heels to step on their passive's dick as well as rounds to consensually torment them.

**D IS FOR D/S.**

D/S refers to supremacy as well as entry, the core of a BDSM partnership. If you take away one reality from this overview, it needs to be that also though the leading companion in D/S connection might be slapping, name-calling, as well as spewing on the passive, BDSM as well as D/S connections are all concerning sexual power exchange, not one individual having power over an additional.

**E IS FOR EDGEPLAY.**

Edgeplay refers to the high-risk crap-- the much more forbidden (or baddest bitch, depending on that you're speaking to) end of the range of BDSM tasks. You do not have actually to obtain impaired to appreciate BDSM.

**F IS FOR FISTING.**

When somebody sticks their whole clenched fist inside a vaginal canal (or butthole), fisting is. Yes, it really feels excellent, and also no, it will not "destroy" anything yet your wish for vanilla sex. Usage lube.

**G IS FOR GOLDEN SHOWERS.**

A gold shower is when you adoringly bath your companion with your piss. It's high time for the BDSM area redeemed this word back from Donald Trump, that, might I advise you, supposedly paid sex employees to pee on a bed that Obama rested in out of spite.

**H IS FOR HARD LIMITS.**

Difficult limitations are sex-related acts that are off-limits. Every person has their very own, as well as you need to review these limits prior to any kind of BDSM play. Utilize it in a sentence: "Please do not pee on me; gold showers are among my difficult restrictions.".

## I IS FOR IMPACT PLAY.

Influence play describes any type of effect on the body, such as paddling, caning, flogging, slapping, and so on

## . J IS FOR JAPANESE BONDAGE.

One of the most widely known kind of Japanese chains is Shibari, in which one companion lock up the various other in complex as well as attractive patterns making use of rope. It's a techni□ue of restriction, however additionally an art type.

## K IS FOR KNIFE PLAY.

Blade play is, well, blade sex. Commonly blade play does not in fact entail attracting blood, yet is done much more for the emotional excitement, such as moving a blade along a companion's body to generate an adrenaline thrill.

## L IS FOR LEATHER.

The BDSM area appreciates natural leather as long as you would certainly anticipate. Natural leather shorts, natural leather paddles, and also natural leather bodices are preferred, although progressively stores give vegan alternatives for their animal-loving nerds.

## M IS FOR MASOCHIST.

A masochist is a person that gets off on obtaining sex-related discomfort.

## N IS FOR NEEDLE PLAY.

, needle play implies utilizing needles on a companion. The majority of expert dommes have customers that are or ask for right into needle play. It can entail sticking a needle (momentarily) with an erotic area such as the nipple area or ... BACK AWAY NOW IF YOU'RE QUEASY ... the shaft of the penis.

## O IS FOR ORGASM DENIAL.

Climax rejection is next-level sex-related expectancy for those that like a pain clitoris or a boner that's been tough for life simply passing away to obtain off-- which is to claim, virtually everybody. The leading companion will usually bring the passive close or to the edge of climax, after that quit.

## P IS FOR PAINSLUT.

A painslut is a dope-ass passive that recognizes what they desire, which's discomfort, dammit.

## Q IS FOR QUEENING.

Queening is when a female, a.k.a. the ☐ueen you should praise, rests on your face. It's simply a glam name for face-sitting, typically utilized in D/S play. Occasionally the ☐ueen will certainly rest on her passive's face for like, hrs.

## R IS FOR RACK.

SHELF means Risk Aware Consensual Kink, which are the BDSM area standards on exactly how to ensure everybody understands the threats they grant. One more collection of standards are the "SSC," which emphasizes maintaining tasks "risk-free, rational, as well as consensual." We kinksters desire everybody to rejoice as well as satisfied, as well as just experience discomfort that they prefer-- without real damage.

**S IS FOR SWITCH.**

A button is somebody that delights in both the passive as well as leading duty. Obtain thee a lady that can do both.


**T IS FOR TOPPING FROM THE BOTTOM.**

A passive man might begin yelping at his domme that she's not making him scent her feet specifically like he desires. It can additionally be component of the scene itself, such as if the passive is roleplaying as a little woman with her dad (this is called "age play").


**U IS FOR URINATION.**

Peing ways peeing (duh) and also in addition to pissing on a passive's face or in their mouth you can do various other awesome and also consensual points with pee, like fill an injection as well as infuse it up somebody's butt! I am not a clinical physician.


**V IS FOR VANILLA.**

Vanilla describes a person (or sex) that is not kinky. If you're vanilla, it's all right. You're typical and also can still locate significant love as well as partnerships regardless of just how much culture courts you.

### W IS FOR WARTENBERG WHEEL.

A Wartenberg Wheel is a cool little steel pinwheel that you can run over your companion's nipple areas or various other erotic areas. It can be made use of as component of clinical play (medical professional proclivity) or simply for the heck of it.

### Y IS FOR YES!

BDSM is everything about passionate authorization. The leading companion will not step on their passive's head and after that push it right into a bathroom without a large ole' "yes, please!".

### Z IS FOR ZENTAI.

Zentai is a skintight Japanese body fit normally constructed from spandex and also nylon. It can cover the whole body, consisting of the face. Dancing professional athletes or groups might put on Zentai, however some individuals get off on the experience of having their whole body bound in limited material, and also use it for kinky factors.

# WHAT A DADDY DOM/LITTLE GIRL RELATIONSHIP IS REALLY LIKE

Align 100 D/s sets alongside. Everyone does it a little in various methods. No 2 sets are especially alike; there are incredibly number of "criteria" in D/s different aside from staying safe in addition to regularly obtaining authorization.

Identifying this, it's a little unreasonable of me to state that Daddy Doms (or Mommies) in addition to little women (or young children), far better called DD/lg, remain in some means numerous from numerous other D/s links. Because I exercise this type of link myself, I can educate you that there are some mediocrity in DD/lg that can develop these links besides different other power exchange attributes. Whether you're interested concerning this vivid or worried that the "hardcore" D/s links aren't for you, it's superb to comprehend a few of the crucial differences.

As well as likewise certainly, you can exercise this type of Dominance as well as likewise access without ever utilizing the term "Daddy" or "little.".

## DD/LG: KINDER, GENTLER FORM OF D/S.

When people ask me to make clear the difference in between DD/lg as well as likewise D/s links, I declare it's a kinder, gentler sort of D/s. Exist different other power exchanges where the Dominant isn't truly rigorous along with the passive has a great deal of adaptability without calling themselves DD/lg?

Yes, littles are expected to take note of their Dominants, do what they're educated, as well as likewise abide by the policies., we may be sent to a side, made to head to bed formerly, or denied some pleasurable incentive that fits with our little character.

While plants, floggers, as well as additionally rope come from my collaboration as a masochist as well as additionally a passive that gets a kick out of chains, I also have stuffies, blankies, Disney movies, in addition to captivating jammies because these factors allow me to enter an area where I feel my most babygirl self. My buddy is frequently Dominant, along with in my mind, regularly Daddy, yet when he joins me in these jobs or gives light ideas for routines in addition to tasks, he's utilizing a gentler part of his nature.

## Doms are Nurturers; Littles Want to Be Cared For.

What often develops the DD/lg (or different other sex versions) along with what people take into consideration the "regular" D/s link is the suggests the power exchange takes place. In various D/s collaborations, a Dominant supplies a command, develops a task, or has a presumption for his/her passive, which is established as well as provided by the passive. The variables for this vary, yet while it may be to help the passive complete a favored goal, result, or uncover new habits, one aspect regularly stated is that it pleases the Dominant

At the similar time, a little could have a deep demand to be taken therapy of. A little wishes to be ruined, placed in at night in addition to used policies to stick to (although we could endure them), among numerous other factors.

In some attributes, the little does not "deal" the Dominant, especially if (or while) they connect to an information age. They do what they're notified. They take notice of their Dominant, yet they are not regularly employed to prepare or take for needs therapy of their Dominant likewise numerous other power exchange collaborations require.

## THE RULES AREN'T AS STRICT.

I'm both a little as well as likewise a passive. The Daddy Dom (or grown-up number) recognizes what's finest for the little (or juvenile number), as well as additionally generates plans as well as additionally criteria with this in mind. This is not various to different other D/s links, yet the huge difference remains in the activity

In lots of D/s links, obedience without query - as quickly as authorization is established - is prepared for. While there are effects for these tasks, littles are rarely, if ever, identified "unfavorable submissives" for this activities.

## WHINING IS (SOMETIMES) OK.

Can it be used also much as well as likewise create difficulties in a DD/lg link? If I'm whining in addition to having a bad day concerning my plans, my going to sleep, or my life in standard, I similarly identify that my Daddy Dom will definitely comfort me or search for ways to attract me out of my unfavorable mindset. A paddling frequently operates for me.

Because of the reality that Daddy Doms are Dominants, one look, a specific tone, or a word can make additionally one of the most challenging little consume our words in addition to meekly reply, "Yes, Daddy" (or "Yes, Mommy"). Great deals of submissives in numerous other D/s links can not picture "disputing" or whining concerning a widely known plan or treatment. The juvenile routines of a little virtually guarantees yawping at some point.


## PLAYFULNESS IS ENCOURAGED.

I would definitely never ever before state that numerous other D/s links do not have their extremely own level of playfulness. We're people in links, in addition to a sensation of wit or getting a kick out of a laugh with each other does not come from any kind of kind of one group of people

Lots Of Daddy Doms have what their friends would absolutely call their "little side". Merely as I acquire in contact with my even more younger self when having fun with my young people, a Daddy Dom faucets right into that part of himself when spending time with a little that's in a vibrant mindset. Being perky at the wrong time usually acquires a little in trouble, as well as likewise possibly sent to the side or their room, which is no satisfying for anyone

Age play is a predisposition that can show up equivalent to the DD/lg collaboration. For countless people that phone call ourselves Daddies, Mommies along with littles, it's not worrying sex. If we're blessed enough to find someone that permits us be our nurturing or childlike selves, establishes a power exchange link with us, in addition to is an individual we prefer to fuck, we generally consider ourselves incredibly lucky.

## BEING A DADDY OR LITTLE ISN'T ABOUT CHILDREN

Ever before listen to a person call their companion "Daddy" as well as really feel a little grossed out? Does the suggestion of a grown-up recognizing as a "little" make you Question what's incorrect with them or Question what that also suggests? While there are some unwell individuals on the planet, the Daddy/little dynamic in D/s partnerships has nothing to do with kids, pedophilia, or "Daddy problems."

Keep in mind: I call my Dominant companion "Daddy" as well as he calls me "babygirl." As a result of options we've made in our connection, we just utilize these names when we're alone, can not be heard, or remain in a team of fellow kinksters. Just how other individuals pick to take care of the titles they make use of is an individual choice.

The Daddy Dom/little lady (or young boy) (DD/lg) vibrant in supremacy as well as entry is usually misinterpreted, also by those within the BDSM way of living. For those that determine as a Daddy or a little, it has absolutely nothing to do with youngsters. It usually has extremely little to do with age or age play either.

### What are Daddy Doms and also Littles?

Eventually, no issue just how bratty or sexy a little is, Daddy is in fee. The vibrant in between a Daddy Dom as well as a little is typically a lot more lively than various other D/s pairings. They keep control, established guidelines, and also normally, maintain a little on their toes.

Others might attach with several ages more youthful than their organic age. For me, my little side is a spirited, more youthful, a lot more prone variation of the lady I offer to the public. If you just pay interest to stereotypes, littles are bratty, love radiance, as well as obsess over Hello Kitty.

The point concerning these tags is that they do not truly issue. That's why I such as BDSM. You can take the components that make feeling to you as well as your companion, fit them right into your one-of-a-kind dynamic, as well as leave the remainder behind.

The Difference Between Age Play as well as the Relationship Dynamic

Both companions take on details duties, one of which is a person of a more youthful age, to satisfy a sex-related dream. Age gamers in a connection determine either as the older nurturer that leads, overviews, as well as educates (Daddies as well as Mommies), or the more youthful, extra childish companion that is provided the liberty to give up particular duties (littles). Neither the connection or the twist are regarding desiring to have sex with kids.

Of program, you can desire the partnership as well as not desire the age play. Some individuals think you can be a Daddy or a little as well as not consider on your own a Dominant or a passive. If it's simply regarding calling your companion Daddy as well as tinting (or whatever little task you choose) or on the various other side, being indulgent and also supporting with your little however having no policies, after that no, there's most likely really little BDSM included.

If the Daddy is in cost as well as makes policies and also the little is meant to follow by those guidelines, you, my good friend, are in a variation of a D/s connection. It may be D/s-light, however you've obtained a Dominant (Daddy) and also a passive (little) as well as policies (technique).

What the DD/lg Dynamic is Really About - From My Perspective

For me to inform you what being in a Daddy Dom/little connection is "truly" like can just come with the prism of my very own point of view and also experience. It does aid that babygirls and also littles have a tendency to have some kind of gravitational pull in between them. Since of that, I've made several close friends in the DD/lg area as well as saw a couple of DD/lg partnerships myself.

Everybody is various, yet the greatest commonness in between Daddies is a re□uirement (not desire, not wish, a demand) to shield, care for, support, and also make life much better for their little. On the various other end of the range, to enable your babygirl or little side to come forth needs depend on and also the desire to be at risk.

The convenience that comes from being enabled to be foolish, do points that make us appear childlike, as well as lean and also depend on somebody that desires just the finest for us is a frustrating sensation. Since of their childish nature, it appears particularly crucial for babygirls as well as littles.

When you're on the outdoors looking in at a partnership, as well as you listen to somebody call their companion "Daddy," do not make presumptions regarding what they're doing or what it indicates. Understand that for several of us, "Daddy" is merely one more title for our Dominant.

# THE DIFFERENCE BETWEEN BDSM AND ABUSE

BDSM, a phrase for "chains, sadomasochism, entry, as well as discipline/dominance" is typically misconstrued by the public. Among one of the most typical misunderstandings is that BDSM threatens, careless, and also violent. When exercised effectively, BDSM is really various than intimate companion misuse.

## WHAT IS BDSM?

For years, BDSM experts have actually kept that twist is secure, rewarding, as well as can favorably impact both an individual's libidos and also their wellness. Over the last couple of years, scientific research has actually validated these insurance claims.

Current researches have actually discovered the many health and wellness advantages of BDSM. Scientists have actually located that those that take part in BDSM tasks have much better psychological health and wellness, even more contentment in their partnerships, as well as much less stress and anxiety than their vanilla-sex e□uivalents.

Those not familiar with BDSM were amazed by a research study from Northern Illinois University, which disclosed that those associated with BDSM are a lot more consent-minded when it concerns sex acts as well as much less most likely to comply with habits related to rape society. Experts of BDSM showed "dramatically reduced degrees of humane sexism, rape misconception approval, as well as victim-blaming."

Research study has actually discovered that those that participate in BDSM are more probable to appreciate the borders of their companion, as well as are much less most likely to go across the limits of individual security.

Although researches reveal that BDSM plainly has favorable advantages, numerous that check out these severe actions from the outdoors regard this sort of sex-related habits as violent, disorderly, as well as unmanageable. Violent habits should never ever become part of the BDSM dynamic, yet just how can we discriminate?


## APPROVAL DIFFERENTIATES BDSM FROM ABUSE

Permission is the foundation of all BDSM task, as well as it's one of the significant elements that distinguishes it from sexual assault.

***In other words, BDSM is consensual. Abuse is not.***

Prior to each BDSM "scene," individuals reveal as well as discuss their sort, needs, and also restrictions. This indicates that all associated with the agreed-upon sex act collection particular objectives identifying what they wish to leave the session-- both psychologically as well as literally.

They likewise review what are described as "soft and also tough restrictions." Difficult restrictions are the points you would certainly never ever involve in, while soft restrictions are points you may experiment with if and also when the time really feels. Having fun with the borders of soft restrictions calls for much deeper settlement before starting a session.

In some cases individuals compose out an agreement describing what is particularly permitted and also prohibited. They after that talk about each product independently, suggesting which is a restriction or a wish.

### BDSM Is Safe, Sane, and also Consensual

Those associated with BDSM commonly utilize the expression "risk-free, rational, and also consensual" to define their sort of sex play. Any kind of play that is specified as "twist" however does not include the agreed-upon risk-free, consensual as well as rational components might □uite possibly be violent.

Safe implies individuals have actually taken preventative measures to reduce dangers. It likewise suggests that individuals are well-informed regarding the devices and also methods being made use of, which can get rid of both undesirable worry and also unsafe habits.

Rational shows that those included remain in a state that enables them to divide dream from truth. This additionally suggests soberness; actions as well as detects are not being hindered by the impact of intoxicants. It indicates abstaining from enforcing impractical assumptions on your companion.

Authorization implies all events have actually gone over as well as settle on borders. Similarly as vital, permission needs to be on-going. Simply put, if a private dreams to alter their mind regarding any kind of task throughout play they can renegotiate at any moment.

### *Interaction Is Key*

Clear interaction is critical to exercising healthy and balanced BDSM Safewords are basic price in this kind of play and also a significant aspect that distinguishes BDSM from misuse.

A secure word is a word or expression that signifies that a person of the desires either gamers to pause or quit totally. An instance of a safeword could be "red," "banana"-- or any other point you would not generally claim throughout sex or in the context of a scene.

In addition, if a Submissive is gagged or a Dominant's hearing suffers, secure signals can be made use of rather. This could be a motion or something the Submissive keeps in their hand and also goes down indicating their dream to stop the scene.

## ESSENTIAL DIFFERENCES BETWEEN ABUSE AND ALSO BDSM

Kinky play can entail points like penalty, embarrassment, and also splits. This might feel like misuse to an outsider, making it not surprisingly hard to discriminate in between both. When contrasted side by side with BDSM, we can see the plain distinctions.

### *BDSM.*

Pre-planned scenarios, not acting out of temper

The very best rate of interest of the Submissive is remembered

When it's over, both celebrations really feel great


### *Abuuse*

Out-of-control circumstance

Performing out of rage

Despair as well as pity really felt adhering to an episode


Violent episodes run out control scenarios. In healthy and balanced BDSM, a Dominant never ever acts automatically out of rage. Scenes are pre-planned with treatment as well as the most effective passion of the Submissive in mind.

A BDSM scene is developed to leave the individuals really feeling pleased and also great when it's over. In comparison, both the abuser as well as the target really feel unfortunate, upset, or embarrassed complying with a violent episode.

Violent circumstances are typically accompanied by drug abuse or psychological disability. In healthy and balanced BDSM, gamers attempt to decrease anything

that might influence their judgment throughout play--
consisting of using medications or alcohol.


**Abuse in BDSM**

Research studies have actually discovered those
entailed in BDSM are much less most likely to endure
specific kinds of misuse, it can still take place. Violent
warnings in a BDSM partnership or scene are really
comparable to those located in various other kinds of
connections. Some alerting actions consist of:

• overlooking sex-related borders

• non-consensual/non-negotiated spoken or physical
misuse

• regulating habits, consisting of extreme envy

• uncertain severe state of mind swings

• chemical abuse

• use last offers and also are afraid to regulate the
target

• separating the sufferer from friends and family

• a background of violent habits with close calls

If you identify these or various other indications of misuse in your very own BDSM experiences, obtain outdoors assistance. If misuse happens at a public BDSM occasion, look for out a Designated or Dungeon Monitor (DM).

If misuse is taking place in your continuous BDSM partnership, you can obtain the solutions of a kink-friendly specialist, misuse assistance hotline, or solution. Call authorities if you locate on your own in prompt risk.

# CONCLUSION

Sex isn't a need or an automated end outcome of BDSM play. You do not have to such as every component of BDSM to live the way of living. Whatever done under the BDSM umbrella, as you will certainly see later on in this overview, drops within a range from light to hefty play.

There's a great deal of info to absorb concerning BDSM whether you're right into light paddlings or full-on natural leather equipment, whips, as well as chains. There are just a few real rules in BDSM:

Approval is whatever. Without permission, it's not BDSM or kinky; - it's misuse.

BDSM needs sincere and also open interaction or it will not function.

When you attempt brand-new points, be secure and also recognize the threats.

There is no person appropriate method to do BDSM. Every person desires as well as has various preferences something various.

Allow's evaluate a little what you've found out and also checked out:

- Sex is not a demand in BDSM.

- You can be a top, a base, or a button. This can transform with various companions.

- Dominance as well as entry (D/s) is a partnership condition within BDSM - sex-related or otherwise.

- You can book BDSM for the bed room just or, similar to D/s, make it a part of your life.

- The twists you like today might be various with time.

- Everyone ought to have a secure word to utilize - a minimum of initially.

All BDSM tasks get on a range from light to hefty, and all are reputable acts of BDSM.

If you keep in mind absolutely nothing else, constantly remember this: your twist isn't my twist, yet your twist is OKAY.

What consenting grownups make with and also per various other is in between them alone, as well as does not impact your kinky play. Do what you appreciate, constantly keep in mind the policies, as well as identify that you are as well as what you such as in the large, enjoyable, and also kinky globe of BDSM.

BDSM is a collection of methods that can happen in or out of a well established partnership. Sex isn't a need or an automated end outcome of BDSM play. You do not have to such as every component of BDSM to live the way of living. Whatever done under the BDSM umbrella, as you will certainly see later on in this overview, drops within a range from light to hefty play.

# DISCLAIMER

This book is not intended as a substitute for the medical advice of physicians. The reader should regularly consult a physician in matters relating to his/her health and particularly with respect to any symptoms that may require diagnosis or medical attention.

The methods describe within this eBook are the author's personal thoughts. They are not intended to be a definitive set of instructions for this project. You may discover there are other methods and materials to accomplish the same end result.

(BDSM, Self-help)

**Do Not Go Yet; One Last Thing To Do**
If you enjoyed this book or found it useful, I'd be very grateful if you'd post a short review on Amazon. Your support does make a difference, and I read all the reviews personally so I can get your feedback and make this book even better.

***Thanks again for your support!***